Kalarippayattu

The complete guide to Kerala's ancient martial art

Kalarippayattu

CHIRAKKAL T. SREEDHARAN NAIR

WESTLAND
NON·FICTION

WESTLAND
NON·FICTION

First published by westland ltd in 2007

Published by Westland Non-Fiction, an imprint of Westland Books, a division of Nasadiya Technologies Private Limited, in 2024

No. 269/2B, First Floor, 'Irai Arul', Vimalraj Street, Nethaji Nagar, Alapakkam Main Road, Maduravoyal, Chennai 600095

Westland, the Westland logo, Westland Non-Fiction and the Westland Non-Fiction logo are the trademarks of Nasadiya Technologies Private Limited, or its affiliates.

ISBN: 9789357765862

10 9 8 7 6 5 4 3 2

Typeset by Trinity Designers & Typesetters and Jojy Philip

Printed at Thomson Press India Private Limited

DEDICATED

TO MY MASTERS AND TO POSTERITY

CONTENTS

INTRODUCTION

Chirakkal T. Sreedharan Nair (1909-1984), our father and the author of this book, was the third son of His Highness C.K. Rama Varma Valiya Raja of Chirakkal Kovilakam and Thayil Kalyanikutty Kettilamma.

The author at 21

While in his teens, Sreedharan Nair took a keen interest in several fitness activities including weight-training, body-building and wrestling.

He started learning *kalarippayattu*, Kerala's martial art, when he was twenty-one. Contrary to the usual custom, he did not enroll himself as a student in a *kalari*. Instead, he was privileged to have several masters of *payattu* to teach him at home.

It was believed that one needed many years to learn the various stages of *payattu*. But Sreedharan Nair, propelled by a single pursuit of perfection, learnt and mastered all the fourteen series in *maippayattu* within a month; the nine advanced series in *otta payattu* in a fortnight; and all the five series in *mara pitichu kuntha payattu* in a matter of one week.

According to him, the mental alertness and physical agility of a student and the expertise of a guru who is willing to teach unreservedly are of prime importance in a *payattu* training programme. From his personal experience as a student of *payattu* and as a well-known *payattu* master, Sreedharan Nair claimed and proved that any able-bodied and keen student could learn all the stages of *payattu* within a matter of months.

He was a non-conformist. He believed that there was nothing mystical or esoteric in *payattu*. It was an excellent self-defence martial art and it ought to be made available to anyone interested in learning it. With this in view, Sreedharan Nair founded Rajkumar Kalari in 1935 at Chirakkal in North Malabar. There, he taught a large number of youngsters. Then, in 1948, he established the Sree Bharat Kalari at nearby Valapattanam, where hundreds of boys and girls were taught *payattu* and many are undergoing training now.

He wrote and published a series of articles on *kalarippayattu* and allied subjects from 1930 onwards. He gave radio talks. He and his disciples presented *payattu* demonstrations at various literary and cultural meetings in Kerala, Tamil Nadu and Karnataka. He taught anyone interested in learning this martial art.

For attempting thus to demystify *payattu* he was regularly attacked, ridiculed and branded by some of the gurus of that time as one who had committed a sacrilege.

According to them the techniques of this martial art were to be kept a closely guarded secret, to be personally handed down only to a chosen few. That was the centuries-old practice. And that was why many of the techniques had either gone into oblivion or died with the gurus.

Sreedharan Nair made it his mission to popularise *payattu* as an ideal martial art form and to prove its relevance as an excellent self-defence technique and a fitness activity that would outlive the guru.

In 1963 when his exhaustive book, *Kalarippayattu,* in Malayalam was published, Father had the satisfaction of having achieved his life's mission. In fact, no one had documented *payattu* so successfully ever before or after.

In 1980 Pervez Merwanji, a Bombay-based award-winning movie maker, held a series of discussions with Father about making a documentary film on *kalarippayattu*. Apparently, Mervanji was so charmed by Father's attitude to life, his candid views and erudition that the movie eventually shaped up as a half-hour documentary on him! Mervanji's film entitled *Way of the Malabar Warrior* was released in France in 1981.

Sreedharan Nair was a unique amalgam of practitioner, master, research scholar and author. He was an undisputed authority on every aspect of this martial discipline and became a legend in his lifetime.

Mythology

Parashurama, the mythical warrior sage, is presumed to have reclaimed the land of Kerala and parts of Konkan from the Arabian sea as a new settlement for sixty-four Brahmin families. Out of them, thirty-two families were settled in Kerala. Parashurama who had mastered the art of armed combat and archery under Lord Siva, taught these arts to twenty-one disciples in the new land that he had reclaimed. He and his disciples are believed to have then established one hundred and eight *kalaris* in different parts of Kerala.

Historians say that a wave of Aryan settlers had moved into the Konkan region and eventually into Kerala some three thousand years ago. Those settlers belonged to the Bhargava Gothra, the clan named after Bhargava or Parashurama. Their cultural, religious and social practices took root in the land of Kolathiri in the far north of Malabar.

Some hold the view that the Parashurama who is believed to have established the first *kalaris* is not a mythological charactor, but one of the early leaders of the Bhargava clan. They cite it as an example of how historical facts distorted by flights of fancy of succeeding generations, could get transformed, even elevated, to the level of myth.

Evolution

Mythology apart, the origin of *payattu* remains shrouded in mystery. No archaeologist, historian or sociologist has succeeded in producing any conclusive theory or view about the century and place where *kalarippayattu*, as a martial art, evolved and how it grew. However, theories abound.

Hunting (*naayaattu*) which had developed almost to the level of a ritual in Kerala, had established its own terminology for hunters to communicate with one another about their quarry and positioning. They followed a highly disciplined ethical code while employing their skills. Perhaps, *payattu* borrowed and adapted several of those skills and the ethical code from the hunters of yore.

Another theory of evolution points to the migration of Aryans. It is believed that some of the Aryans who migrated to the south of India, eventually settled in the Konkan region and Kerala. They might have brought with them several forms of art and culture and also techniques of fighting from the *dhanur veda*. The people of Kerala must have imbibed some of them and adapted and interwoven them with their own techniques that evolved as *payattu*.

The long arduous journey of generations through centuries and the synthesis of various types of martial arts from different parts of India might have eventually crystallised into *kalarippayattu* as we know it.

And Kerala cherished and nurtured it as its own.

Archaeologists, historians and sociologists may probe deeper and come up with more views and theories about the century and place where *kalarippayattu*, as a martial art evolved and how it grew. However, for the present, the origin of *payattu* remains in the realms of mythology and mystery.

History

According to some historians, it was during the Sangam Age (circa BC 200–600 AD) *kalarippayattu* evolved and developed. Tamil literature and anthologies describe the warring tribes of that period. The word *kalari* is used for a battlefield and an arena for training in weaponry. The tribals (men and women) were trained in wielding weapons including the sword (*val*), spear (*vel*), bow (*vil*) and shield (*khedam*); and they were ferocious in battle.

The period between the 7th and 9th centuries was the Brahminical Age in Kerala. The Brahmins established their supremacy and influenced every sphere of the society. They set up centres called *salais* for training in the vedas and warfare.

The Perumals (or Cheras) ruled Kerala from the 8th century to the 11th century. The Chera rulers patronised *kalaris* and established a fighting force with a core group of one thousand Nayar (or Nair) captains. And each captain had ten well-trained soldiers (or *Chekons*) under his command.

The Cheran rule (8th to 11th century) overlapped a part of the Brahminical Age (7th to 9th century). During the Cheran rule, *salais* continued imparting martial training to Brahmin students, while *kalaris* groomed soldiers belonging to the other castes and groups. By then the Brahmins, having consolidated their domain, chose to remain as landlords and priests. They ceased training themselves in martial arts, but the *salais* continued imparting vedic education. Eventually the *salais* vanished from Kerala. But the *kalaris* continued to function, teaching *payattu*.

The long rule of the Perumals in Kerala came to an end in the early years of the 12th century. The emergence of a number of kings and chieftains wielding almost total control over Kerala, resulted in the fragmentation of Kerala into principalities called *swarupam*. The political and administrative machinery in Kerala had more or less collapsed under the constantly feuding kings and chieftains. For personal benefit, they maintained private armies and mercenaries thoroughly trained in the art of warfare.

One such was the Zamorin (*samoothiri*) of Calicut (Kozhikode). He had a well-structured army under his control. There are records of the armies maintained by the Raja of Pazhashi, the Kolathiri royal family and a few others in Malabar, and others in the southern parts of Kerala.

The fighting readiness of those armies, the valour of the warriors and their expertise in *payattu* and the exploits are graphically described in history books and ballads.

Ballads

The ballads of North Malabar (*vatakkan pattukal*) are believed to have been written between 1500 and 1700. They contain detailed narratives of feuds, describe various techniques used by the experts of *payattu* and document the royal patronage enjoyed by *payattu*.

These ballads as also the *thekkan pattukal* which are the ballads of Southern Kerala, are replete with interesting stories told of the expertise and exploits of *payattu* stalwarts like Mathiloor Gurukkal, Tacholi Othenan, Payyamballi Chandu, Aromal Chekavar, Unni Archa, Chengannuradi, Itanatan and Iravikutty Pilla.

Tacholi Othenan, the undisputed exponent and all time great of *kalarippayattu*, was born in 1584. After his death at the age of thirty-two, the people of Malabar made a cult hero of him and eventually deified and worshipped him as a demi-god.

Payattu, as a highly evolved form of martial art, reached the acme of its popularity in Kerala between the 14th and 16th century.

During this period, in some parts of Kerala, especially in the Malabar region, if the king or chieftain could not satisfactorily settle a dispute between two groups or families, it was settled by an *ankam.* An *ankam* was an armed fight in full view of the village assemblage, between two hired *payattu* experts. The dispute was settled in favour of the group or family whose mercenary emerged victorious. The family of the vanquished mercenary was adequately compensated.

Strangely, the mercenaries did not fight just for the money, but they considered an invitation to fight an *ankam* a social honour.

Poithu was an armed *payattu* combat between two invidivuals to settle their private quarrels. Many thrilling stories of *ankam* and *poithu* combats, which were fairly common then, are poetically narratted in *Vatakkan Pattukal.*

In 1936, a *poithu* was arranged in Calicut. The two combatants were C.V. Narayanan Nair and Chirakkal T. Sreedharan Nair. They were prepared to fight to the finish in front of the public assemblage, to prove who possessed superior skills in *payattu.* Just as the combat was about to begin, the judges announced that the Government had denied permission for such a combat. Therefore, would the combatants demonstrate their skills in *payattu* in a 'friendly' fight? That friendly demonstration did not take place, as the two Nairs were there to fight to the finish, not to entertain the assemblage. Both of them in private always admired each other's skill in *payattu.*

Under the patronage of the royal families of Malabar, a number of *kalaris* were established in each and every village, and each of them functioned under the direct supervision of a guru. Irrespective of caste, community, sex, religion and social status, the people of Kerala learnt the art of *payattu.*

The ballads of North Malabar tell stories of experts in *kalarippayattu* going to Tulu Nadu to learn and hone their skill in some of the more advanced techniques of sword fighting. To those who were training themselves for *ankam* and *poithu*, the Tulu Nadan techniques of *payattu* were important.

The State of Karnataka, of which Tulu Nadu is a part, had a well-developed form of martial art called *garadi.* Upto a century or so ago, that martial discipline was widely practiced. And there must have been regular interaction between the experts of *payattu* from Malabar and those of *garadi* from Tulu Nadu.

During the reign of Udaya Varma of the Kolathiri royal family (circa 1300-1333), two hundred and thirty-seven Brahmin families from Tulu Nadu were brought and given settlements in North Malabar. They fairly quickly seeped into the socio-cultural fabric of Malabar with a status and rights equal to that of the Namboothiris. The house of Kolathiri bestowed upon them the right to be priests in all its temples.

Some of those Brahmins from Tulu Nadu are believed to have been experts in the art of warfare following the *garadi* martial system.

Chirakkal T. Sreedharan Nair's father Rama Varma Valiya Raja (1881-1952) of Chirakkal Kovilakam belonged to the Kolathiri royal family.

Influence

It is obvious that *kalarippayattu*, as a highly developed martial art and as an extremely popular physical cultural activity, had a direct bearing on the development of Kerala's art and culture.

The ritualistic folk art forms of *theyyam* and *thira* which are peculiar to Malabar have deified some exponents of *payattu* including Payyamballi Chandu, Tacholi Othenan, Kaari Gurukkal and Mannappan. Year after year, their lore and deeds are enacted as *theyyams* at various *kaavukal* (tribal temples). In order to lend authenticity to the characters, the *theyyam* performers wield different weapons, sing the stories of their exploits and bless the congregation. *Theyyam* and *thira* focus on the cultural rather than the physical aspect of

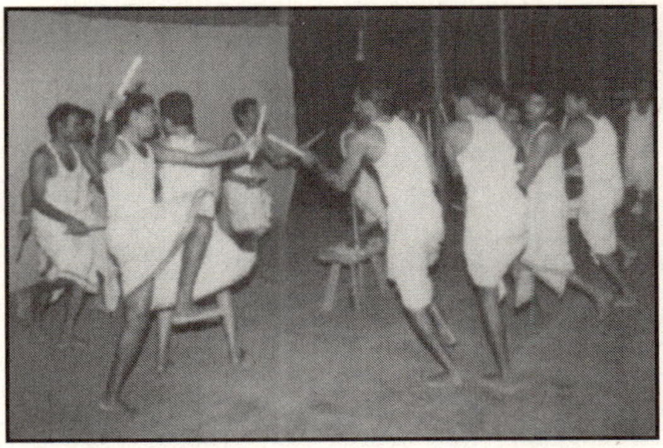

Kolkali

payattu. The songs (*thottam*) are replete with references to certain forms of sorcery taught as part of *payattu*.

The vibrant yet graceful movements of *kolkali* bear striking resemblence to those of *payattu*. While dancing to the tune and rhythm of music, the *kolkali* performers wield the short-staff, thinner and smaller but almost similar in shape to the one used in *payattu*. Their forward and backward movements, the way they lift their legs and kick them in the air and their body movements are almost identical to those of *maithozhil*, while the way they wield the staff is similar to those in *kolthaari* of *payattu*. Recorded evidence shows that *kolkali* was once practised as part of *vattenthirippu* style of *payattu* in Malabar.

Poorakali, a traditional folk dance form prevalent in the extreme north of Malabar, has two distinct and diverse aspects—one intellectual, the other related to dance and physical culture. The direct influence of *kalarippayattu* exercises is evident in the movements of the *poorakali* artistes.

Historical evidence establishes the influence of *kalarippayattu* on *kathakali*, the stylised dance-drama peculiar to Kerala. Kottarakara and Kottayam Thampurans who had choreographed the stories of *kathakali* for the

Poorakali

first time (circa 1600-1700) had borrowed several exercises and movements from *kalarippayattu* and then suitably stylised and adapated them. The contributions of the Raja of Vettath Nadu, who ruled between 1630 and 1640, in choreographing *kathakali* are noteworthy. One of his warriors, Sankaran Nair, an expert in *kalarippayattu* could quickly adapt and stylise his body movements to suit *kathakali*. Most of the early performers of *kathakli* were well-versed in *payattu*. They were the most preferred natural choice as they had already developed the stamina required for the all-night performance of *kathakali*. And they could move with atheletic grace.

The stories enacted in *kathakali* have any number of duels between *deva* and *asura* characters. A knowledge of *payattu* with its kicks, stances, circular movements, quick yet graceful reflexes of limbs and body, and practice in wielding weapons was found very useful.

Likewise, the brisk movements and vibrant pivots of the *yakshagana* artistes of Karnataka State appear to have been adapted and stylised from the *garadi* martial discipline of Tulu Nadu.

In some of the temples of North Malabar, there is a peculiar dance called *nritham* performed by the *Embrandiri* priests who are

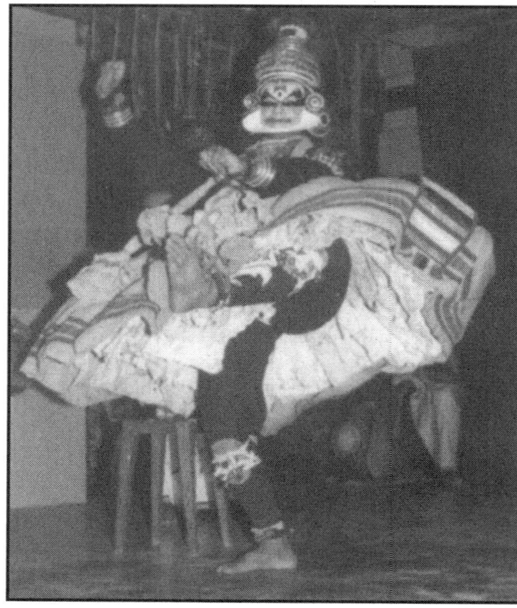

Kathakali

decendants of the Tulu Nadu Brahmins who had settled in North Malabar. They dance carrying decorated idols on their heads. Their steps and movements bear subtle resemblence to those of *payattu*.

There are other ritualistic folk-art forms including *velakali*, *parichamuttukali*, *sangakkali*, *patayani* and *mutiyettu* which are popular in Kerala, which bear striking resemblance to the exercises of *payattu*. The *velakali* performers wield a sword and shield and simulate the movements, steps and stances employed in *kalarippayattu*.

In or about the 20th century, *kalarippayattu* influenced the development of circus too. Here the single-handed efforts of Keeleri Kunhikannan Teacher, who was an expert of *kalarippayattu*, resulted in the establishment of the first ever Circus Training Centre (1901) in Tellicherry in Malabar. Keeleri called his training centre Circus Kalari because he introduced into circus many of the exercises of *maithozhil* and integrated them into acrobatics which enthralled viewers all over the world.

As the popularity of *payattu* expands outside the boundaries of Kerala, the land of its origin, some famous Indian dance choreographers, in recent times, have incorporated a large number of graceful and power-packed movements of *payattu*, especially *maippayattu*, in dances. There are also dance schools and dramatic troupes overseas who use *payattu* movements to defenite advantage.

There are many, including experts in the practice of Karate and Judo, who hold that the Buddhist monks including Bodhidharma, the founder of Zen Buddhism, took Kerala's martial art to China and Japan. Some have paid glowing tributes to *kalarippayattu* calling it "the ancestor of all great Asian martial arts, such as Judo and Karate'. However, no one has been able to produce any conclusive evidence to substantiate this theory.

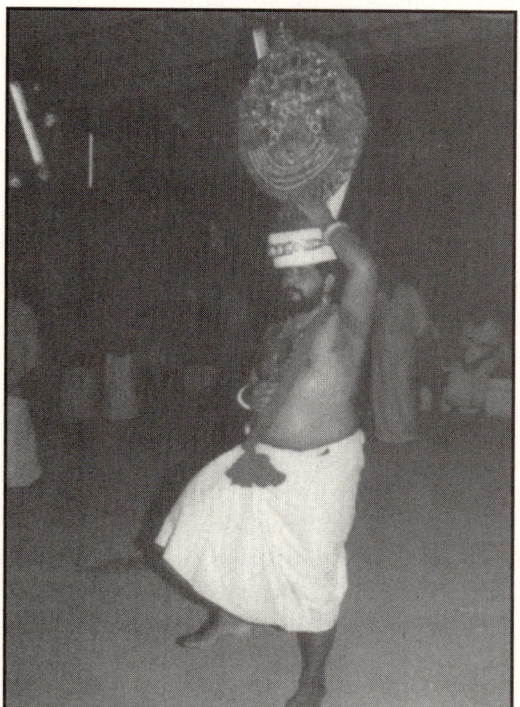

Nritham

Decadance

The Europeans who came to coastal Kerala as travellers and traders towards the close of the 15th century eventually consolidated their political supremacy there. While some of them were appreciative of the highly developed form of martial art popular in Kerala, there were others who saw in it a threat to their sustained supremacy.

The first recorded evidence of the decline of *payattu is* found during the Portuguese rule. The local warriors who were adepts in wielding traditional weapons found them to be ineffective against the fire-spitting weapons of the Portuguese.

The local kings and chieftains who had till then maintained well-trained warriors found it no longer worth their while to continue patronising *kalaris* and maintain an army of men trained in them.

When Marthanda Varma, the ruler of Travancore (circa 1750) modernised his army, the traditional art of warfare and the warriors who wielded traditional weapons were replaced. This single act triggered the decline of *payattu* in South Kerala.

Hyder Ali (1766) and Tippu Sultan (1788) from Mysore invaded Malabar and disturbed the socio-political system there. They were thus indirectly responsible for the decline of *kalarippayattu* as an effective form of warfare and as a popular physical culture activity patronised and nurtured till then by the centuries-old feudal system of Malabar.

During the rule of Hyder Ali and Tippu Sultan even *garadi*, the martial art of Tulu Nadu, sustained a severe blow. In 1799 during the British occupation of Canara (Karnataka State of today) this martial art went into disuse and eventually became extinct.

Pazhassi Raja in his armed revolt against the British (1796-1805) was supported and assisted by his Nair warriors and the Kurichya tribals of Wyanad. The British found it a serious threat to their rule in Malabar. In fact they were already well aware of the Nairs' valour, expertise in wielding weapons and fighting fitness. To curb and contain that revolt and any probable ones in the future, Lord William Bentinck, President and General-in-Council, Fort St. George, Madras issued a government order in 1804 proclaiming a permanent ban on the possession of weapons and weapons training in Malabar.

Anyone who violated Bentinck's order was condemned as a traitor and was either deported for life or given the death penalty. The officials raided house after house and confiscated all arms and ensured that this ban was not violated.

Almost a similar situation was repeated in Travancore as well to curb and contain Veluthampi Dalawa's revolt (1809) against the British.

Even so a few masters continued, though in secrecy, to impart training in *payattu*. Were it not for their ardour and valour this well-entrenched martial art would have been lost to us for ever.

Revival

The one-hundred-and-forty-three-year-old ban on the possession of weapons and weapons training between 1804 and 1947 succeeded in almost totally destroying the popular appeal and the systematic practice of *payattu* all over Kerala. The generations of young men and women who lived during that period were denied the opportunity to learn this unique martial art.

The slow journey of its revival started with the Swadeshi (or Freedom) Movement in Kerala in the early years of the 20th century.

The efforts of K. Kelappan, a well-known nationalist of Malabar who belonged to Vatakara, in reviving *kalarippayattu* are praiseworthy. Equally important were the individual contributions of *payattu* masters including Kottakkal Kanaran Gurukkal, Kadiroor Kunhanbu Gurukkal, Maroli Ramunni Gurukkal, Chemberi Kunhikannan Gurukkal, C.V. Narayanan Nair, Chirakkal T. Sreedharan Nair Nair and a few others.

Chirakkal T. Sreedharan Nair started his first *kalari*—Rajkumar Kalari—in Chirakkal in 1935 and in 1948 he established in Valapattanam the Sree Bharat Kalari which continues to function ever since.

Even after Independence (1947), the Government of India and its officials, unfortunately paid scant attention to *kalarippayattu* and other folk art forms which were forced to remain in hibernation for more than a century.

An organised attempt to revive and popularise *payattu* was started in 1958 with the sponsorship of the Kerala State Sports Council. Under the Council's overall control, the State Kalarippayattu Association was formed with its headquarters in Trivandrum. Currently there are approximately five hundred *kalaris* functioning all over Kerala. Their contribution towards propagating and popularising this martial art is commendable.

In 1999, the Kerala State Government initiated action in establishing Martial Art Training Centres in different districts of the State.

This Book

Published history on the evolution and development of *payattu* and the reproduction of *vaaithaari* (oral command) will help retain the memory of *kalarippayattu* as a martial art. They will not however be able to contribute to the actual application and practice of the diverse *payattu* exercises without the aid of a manual.

In some palmleaf manuscripts, we find *vaaithaari* of *payattu*. However, even one who has already achieved a high level of expertise in *payattu* finds it almost impossible to glean the meaning of the *vaaithaari*, leave alone learn and practise them.

For example, no one now appears to know either to practise or to teach the two most advanced techniques of fighting *puliangam* where the atheletes use the sword and shield and *thatamura* where only the sword is used for attack and defence. Their *vaaithaari* exists, but even experts in *kalarippayattu* are unable to decipher the meanings.

Another glaring example is *urumi* (a long and flexible sword-like weapon) *payattu*. The *vaaithaari* for the exercises with the *urumi* must have existed, presumably. But now it remains lost to us.

Yet another is *kattara* (dagger, improvised flat metalic version of *otta* baton) *payattu*. Here also the traditional *vaaithaari* is non-existant. Hence this is not included in this book. However, many are found to practice this with a few exercises adapted from *otta*.

In this book, Sreedharan Nair, has taken pains to explain each and every exercise in *kalarippayattu*. No one has so far attempted to do this. It is a Manual, not just another book on *payattu*.

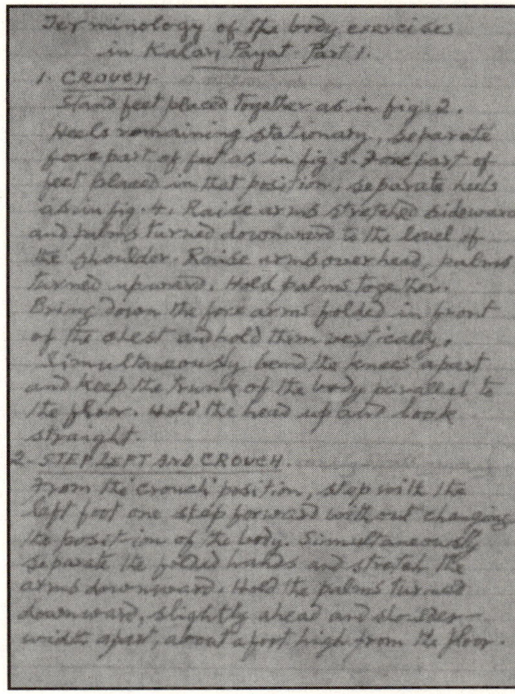

Terminology of the body exercises
in Kalari Payat Part 1.
1. CROUCH
Stand feet placed together as in fig. 2.
Heels remaining stationary, separate
fore part of feet as in fig 3. Fore part of
feet placed in that position, separate heels
as in fig. 4. Raise arms stretched sideward
and palms turned downward to the level of
the shoulder. Raise arms overhead, palms
turned upward. Hold palms together.
Bring down the fore arms folded in front
of the chest and hold them vertically.
Simultaneously bend the knees apart
and keep the trunk of the body parallel to
the floor. Hold the head up and look
straight.
2. STEP LEFT AND CROUCH.
From the 'crouch' position, step with the
left foot one step forward without changing
the position of the body. Simultaneously
separate the folded hands and stretch the
arms downward. Hold the palms turned
downward, slightly ahead and shoulder-
width apart, about a foot high from the floor.

Author's handwritten manuscript

For a period of nine years from 1956, Father was the resident teacher of *kalarippayattu* at the Y.M.C.A. College of Physical Education in Madras. While there, he had taught *payattu* to a large number of students from all over India and some from Nepal, Sri Lanka and African countries. The medium of instruction was English. It was there that he wrote the first draft of this book, and after a few more drafts the MS went into years of hibernation.

Sreedharan Nair created this book from his experience as a practitioner and teacher of *payattu* spread over five decades.

We, his two sons, learnt *payattu* under Sreedharan Nair's direct guidance. We had the privilege of assisting him in reworking on the several drafts of this book and in determining its final format.

While the contents of this book are his, the photographs which appear in the pages are prepared under our direction, many years after he passed away.

Father had desired that this book in English, meant for a global audience, be published one day. In fulfilling that desire, his book is being published now. And through this, we perpetuate our father's memory and the outstanding contribution that he made to this unique martial art. Were he alive, nothing else would have pleased him more than to see his life's work in print.

S.R.A. DAS
S.R.D. PRASAD
Shakti Bhavan
Chirakkal Post
Kannur 670 011, Kerala
INDIA
e-mail: sindhukdas@gmail.com
srd_prasad@yahoo.com
Phone: 9446015814

PART ONE

KALARI – THE GYMNASIUM

The *kalari* is traditionally a thatched shed where boys and girls are trained in the martial art of *payattu.* It was customary for people in Kerala to send their children to a *kalari* when they were about seven; but any able-bodied person, irespective of his age, can learn *kalarippayattu*, and attain considerable proficiency and expertise.

Earth is dug out to a depth of about three feet from a rectangular plot of ground measuring forty-two feet in length in an east-westerly direction and twenty-one feet in breadth. The dug-up soil is piled around the pit and rammed into strong ridges. The floor is also levelled and rammed. The area is thatched-roofed with the support of two main pillars, one in the east and the other in the west. This *kalari* is called *nalppatheerati kalari* or *ankakkalari.*

In the south-west corner of the *kalari* is the seat of Bhadra, the presiding deity of war. Five tapering quadrant steps erected one above the other at the corner, form a kind of pedestal known as the *poothara.* At the top is a cone made of mud. *Pootharas* with seven and/or nine steps are also found in some *kalaris.*

A small elevated place called *guruthara* lies between the western main pillar and the seat of the presiding deity. It is constructed in memory of the ancient preceptors who were instrumental in the evolution of the martial art. There are some who look upon it as the seat dedicated to Parameswara, the Hindu God of the Universe. *Poothara* and *guruthara* are considered sacred.

The entrance to the *kalari* is on the east, to the right of the main pillar. A flight of steps lead one down to the floor of the *kalari.* The ridges on the right and left of the entrance, serve as seats for spectators. The roof and the sides are neatly covered with plaited palm leaves; the entrance is left uncovered.

Besides this type of *kalari* called *nalppatheerati-kalari*, there are various others of different dimensions known as *anpatheerati kalari* (or *netumkalari*), *muppatheerati kalari* (or *thotukalari*), *pathinetteerati kalari* (or *kurumkalari*) and *pantheerati kalari* (or *cherukalari*).

Kalari Customs and Conventions

The training commences on an auspicious day. The *kalari* presents a festive look. It is decorated with arches and festoons. The area in and around the *kalari* is kept clean.

The *poothara* and *guruthara* are decorated with flowers and a traditional lamp is lit. Plantains, popped rice and flowers are placed in front of the presiding deity. The atmosphere is filled with the fragrance of burning incense and camphor.

The guru (as the *payattu* teacher is called) enters the *kalari* with his right foot first, bows with devotion to the presiding deity, chants the mantra OM, and reverently places one handful of flowers on the *poothara*, and another on the *guruthara.* After worshipping the presiding deity and the preceptors, the guru adores the *ashtadikpalas*, the Lords of the eight directions.

Each day the class begins with the placing of flowers on the *poothara* and the *guruthara.* When the training for the day is over and the pupils have gone home, the guru sits before the *poothara* and the *guruthara* and worships the presiding deity and his teachers. These customs and conventions are observed in all *kalaris* with minor variations.

A pupil enters the *kalari* with his right foot first. Then he bows before the *poothara* and the *guruthara*. He begins the day's training after paying obeisance to the guru by touching his feet. He repeats this after he finishes the day's training.

At the end of the annual course pupils display their ability and skill in the art of *kalarippayattu* before an invited assemblage. Before the pupils leave the *kalari* after completing their course, they offer *dakshina*, the customary fees, to the guru.

Traditionally *kalarippayattu* was taught only during the rainy season. But now classes are conducted all through the year. It is not essential that classes be conducted only inside a traditionally built *kalari*. A well-ventilated gymnasium or open playground will adequately serve the purpose.

A tight cloth (supporter) known as *kacha* or *langotti* is worn to gird up the loins during workout sessions.

The trainees in a *kalari* apply medicated oil on their body before beginning the day's workout. It protects the skin, helps keep the body warm and reduces the fatigue.

During the training period, the pupil goes through a course of body massage with medicated oil. Normally the massage, which lasts a fortnight, is done by the guru.

From practical experience, it is found that oiling the body for the workout is not a must.

STYLES, COMMANDS, PRACTICE

There are regional variations in the styles and the methods of training. In the northern part of Kerala, three different styles are prevalent: *arappukkai, pillathangi* and *vattenthirippu.*

Techniques in *pillathangi* consist of brisk movements of advancing and retreating coordinated with kicking, stretching, trotting and intermittently slapping the floor with both palms. Different methods in wielding weapons are also taught.

In *vattenthirippu*, besides body exercises and defence and attack with staffs and swords, there are also tumbling exercises. This *payattu* style includes *kolkali* which is a group activity stressing on recreational aspects.

Some information on *kalarippayattu* is available in the palmleaf manuscripts, RANGA-BHYASAM and VERUMKAIPITUTHAM at the Oriental Manuscript Library in Madras. No mention about the authors and the period of these manuscripts is made. The techniques mentioned are obsolete, but there are similarities between some of the body exercises mentioned in RANGABHYASAM and those of the *arappukkai* style of *payattu.*

The style once prevalent in Ponnani Taluk in Malabar is known as *vallabhatta. Otimurisseri* is a style that existed in central Kerala. In this particular style, combative activities with and without weapons and methods of treatment of cuts, fractures and wounds are included.

The *dronamballi* style of self-defence was prevalent in the southern part of Kerala. Literature on this is available in the University Library, Trivandrum. Besides the art of defence, the techniques of disabling an opponent by occult means or by resorting to the power of mantra are included in this style.

Of all the styles of *payattu*, *arappukkai* is considered the best, and is by far the most popular. The body exercises in this style, consisting of various kinds of high kicks, are superior to the others.

This book deals with the *arappukkai* style.

Oral Commands used in Payattu
(*Payattu Vaaithaari*)

Vaaithaari is the Malayalam word for oral command. Each command is termed as Phase in this book and is explained.

It is difficult, to those who do not know the language, to try and pronounce, leave alone to understand, the Malayalam words. Hence, no transliteration of the Malayalam words in English is attempted in this book. Instead, each *vaaithaari* is suitably changed into English words. It is not an exact translation of the Malayalam words into English.

The few examples given below are meant to clarify the reason why an exact translation or transliteration would have been a futile exercise.

- *Thozhuthamarnnu (tho-zhu-tha-mar-nnu)* can be quite a tongue twister to any non-Malayalee. Used instead is the English expression 'Bow and Crouch'.
- *Valathu nere, athu veethu, athu nere, athu veethu, athu nere* can be quite a mouthful, but 'Swing Right Five Times' will be easily understood.

- *Etuthu nokki etathethu, valathemmal chaati ketti* may serve no useful purpose to a non-Malayalee, but 'Kick Left, Step and Leap' will.

The meaning of some *vaaithaaris* may not be easily understood because of the poetic twist in their construction. For example—

- *othiram chaati vetti* is the poetic structure of *chaati othiram vetti.* In this book the command is 'Hit head pouncing' (*otta,* Phase 1)
- *koote thatuthu pongi patinju katakam*' is the poetic version of '*thatuthu, koote pongi, patinju, katakam*'. The command in English is 'Defend abdomen, Spring up, Squat and Defend ankle' (*otta,* Phase 2).

Vaaithaari is meant to scientifically structure *payattu.* There is nothing mystical in it. Hence, nothing is lost if an appropriate English expression is used instead. If anything, it only helps for clarity.

Vaaithaari in *payattu* is a command to guide a trainee through each phase. Each command is normally given by the guru or master (M) to his pupil (P). The language of the *vaaithaari* is short and crisp to match the speed of the practitioner.

In changing the commands from Malayalam into English and making their meanings clear, great care was taken. However, there could be inadequacies. These could not be helped.

Each and every phase is explained so that anyone who follows the explanation minutely will be able to learn to perform the phases. Yet it cannot be used as 'Self Teacher'. The personal guidance of an expert in *payattu,* at least for a short period of time, is a must.

The phases are grouped under separate *arappu* (series). Each phase in a series should be performed, one after another, to complete the series. Care should be taken that the movements are smooth, yet fast.

The series begins with simple techniques and gradually moves on to more complex ones.

In this book, each Phase is explained separately. Each is given a name and a number for ease of reference. The number in brackets after the name of each Phase corresponds with the number given to it.

Learning and Practising Payattu

Kalarippayattu is learnt in four stages. *Maippayattu* or body exercises form the first stage. Next, one learns to use wooden weapons of different lengths and shapes. After this, one learns to wield sharp weapons including the sword and shield and spear. The fourth and last stage is *verumkai* or bare-handed defence and attack.

All these are included in this illustrated manual under appropriate sections.

Each and every movement in a Phase is explained. Several Phases are grouped together to make up a Set. Many Sets are regrouped to make a Series.

To start with, set a daily time-frame for your training programme. Depending on convenience, you may practise in the morning or evening. Half an hour a day will be adequate for the beginner. You may gradually increase the time. A daily practice session of anything between sixty and ninety minutes is found to be sufficient. Over-exerting oneself is not advisable in a martial art training programme.

Try and learn each Phase carefully and systematically. Once you are sure of each movement in a Phase, coordinate the movements and gradually add grace, force and speed to them.

You are advised to start with *maippayattu*. Start learning the basic postures and phases (p 12, 14). Follow the explanation very minutely. After you have learnt and more or less perfected these basics, start learning Phase 1, Phase 2, Phase 3 and so on. When you have learnt all the Phases in Set A of the First Series, practise them to perfection. It will be helpful to remember and practice the Phases in Sets, because the Sets keep repeating as you progress in your learning programme.

Take care that all the movements in one Phase are coordinated with those of the Phase that follows. Ensure that your movements are graceful and at the same time powerful. Increase the speed and force of your movements as your confidence-level increases.

This will take a few weeks of regular and systematic practice. It is better to progress slowly.

Now you may learn the new Phases which form part of the Second Series. Within a few days, you will have learnt the Second Series as well. At this stage, instead of going on to the Third Series in *maippayattu*, you are advised to try your hand at *pandeeraan veeshal* and *kettukaari*. In either of these, try and learn four or five Phases each day, and practise them in Sets before you move on to the other Phases and Sets. Keep practising all the Phases you have learnt earlier.

While learning the Phases and Series in *kettukaari* and the Phases in *pandeeraan veeshal*, you may for a few minutes each day practise the Series you have already learnt in *maippayattu*.

After you have learnt the first two Series in *kettukaari*, and all the Phases in *pandeeraan veeshal,* you may return to learn the Third and Fourth Series in *maippayattu*.

Thereafter, try your hand at *muchaan*. As the *muchaan* staff is wielded at close range, take extra care not to hurt your sparring partner while practising. Learn a few Phases a day and perfect them. Once you have learnt all the Sets in the First Series, practise them every day till your footwork, body movements, defence and attack are well coordinated. Gradually increase your speed and add force to your attacks.

Return to *maippayattu*. Learn a couple of new Series. Simultaneously, return to *kettukaari* and learn the rest of the Series.

Now that you have already learnt and practised many of the Series in *maippayattu* and *kolethaari*, you may turn your attention to *verumkai*.

As explained earlier, learn each movement in an attack and defence carefully and systematically. Learn one technique at a time and practise it to perfection. Gradually increase the speed and force. Do not rush through the techniques. Remember not to hurt or injure your sparring partner.

After a week of bare-handed defence and attack, you may return to learn more Series in *maippayattu* and *kolethaari*.

You may also, at this stage, learn the Phases dealing with salutation in *maippayattu* and *kolethaari*.

It is also necessary that you repeat all the Series you have already learnt. You may not have the time or energy to repeat all of them on a daily basis. However, practise at least two Series from each stage every day. As you go on, you will find that your movements are much more graceful, more forceful and faster. They ought to be that way, as grace, force and speed are the very essence of *kalarippayattu*. Once you have thoroughly mastered all the Series in *muchaan*, go on to learn the Phases in *otta. Otta* is the most advanced and powerful among wooden weapons. You must see to it that the movements of your body and the *otta* baton are well-coordinated while learning and practising the Phases, Sets and Series. You may learn the First Series in *otta* and perfect your attack and defence.

As you have already understood, *payattu* is learnt and practised as directed and regulated by the *vaaithaari*. However, you should be prepared to defend and attack—in actual combat situations—without following oral commands. To orient your reflexes for actual combat situations, try at random attacks at your sparring partner and defend his attacks. Start very carefully, slowly and increase your speed and force as you go on.

Now you are ready to take the first lessons in wielding sharp weapons.

Start learning a few Phases in *valvali*. Within a few days, you will have learnt all the Phases. Synchronise the movements of your body and the weapons from Phase to Phase and practise them carefully. When you have more or less mastered all the Phases, increase the speed and gradually add force to your cuts and defence. After *valvali*, you take on a sparring partner and learn the Phases and Series in *valppayattu*. Take extra care not to hurt your sparring partner while practising.

You may divide your day's practice session betwen *valppayattu* and *otta*. You may also practise *maippayattu* and *kolethaari*. Another day, you may practise *verumkai*.

You can now handle wooden weapons and the sword and shield. Your body movements have attained a high degree of speed and agility. Your reflexes are quick. You are now ready to learn to wield the spear against one who wields the sword and shield. Go on to learn each Phase, Set and Series of *mara pitichu kuntha payattu*.

Depending on your physical and mental capability, you could learn and reasonably master all the stages in *payattu* within a matter of, say one year. But you are advised to keep practising *payattu* every day. This will keep you mentally alert, physically agile and in excellent health. Keep trying to better your own performance. Constant practice is the only way to achieve perfection.

PART TWO

BODY EXERCISES
(*Maippayattu*)

Maippayattu or body exercises form the foundation of all other exercises in *payattu*. These callisthenics endow one with an agile and supple body, a graceful gait, stamina, strength, ready and quick reflexes of the limbs, balance and stability of footwork.

It is obvious that the preceptors of *payattu* had minutely observed the postures, stances and movements of animals, reptiles and birds. And while developing the different techniques employed in *payattu*, they adapted some of them. There are a few *vativukal* (stances) with names such as *gaja vativu* (elephant stance), *simha vativu* (lion stance), *marjara vativu* (cat stance), *ashva vativu* (horse stance), *sarpa* or *naga vativu* (cobra stance) and *kukkuta vativu* (crane stance).

Payattu vaaithaari (oral command) uses these names to indicate the different techniques employed in defence, attack and averting attacks.

In fact, it is in *maippayattu* that one learns the different stances, pivots, leaps, trots, blocks, cuts, kicks and forward, backward, sideways and circular movements employed in defending and attacking.

In this book, the exercises in *maippayattu* are grouped under fourteen series. Among them, the first to eighth are *maiyirakku* and the ninth to fourteenth are *pakarchakkal*. The exercises in *pakarchakkal* are more advanced, hence more strenuous to practice.

The series begins with simple exercises and gradually moves on to more complex ones.

PRELIMINARY POSTURES AND PHASES

Start practising the following Postures and Phases of *maippayattu* before you start and learn the advanced Phases. These will equip you to learn to perform the more advanced Phases without mistakes and with confidence.

You are advised to repeat each Phase several times, at a stretch and thus perfect the movements. These will serve as very good warming-up exercises. It is normal practice to repeat two Phases, one followed by the next. For example, start with 'Straight Right' and then take 'Straight Left'. Repeat right and left from one end of the *kalari* floor to the other, then turn and repeat to come back to the starting position. After these two, repeat 'Outward Right' and 'Outward Left', 'Inward Right' and 'Inward Left' and so on.

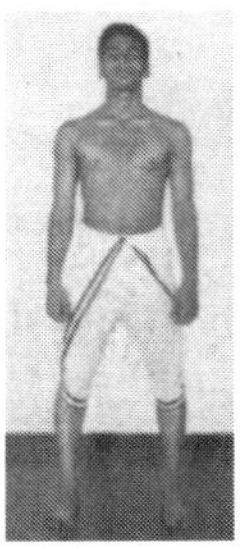

POSTURES

STAND ASTRIDE

Stand upright in a relaxed position, with your feet a shoulder width apart, toes pointing forward. Your arms remain on either side of the body. Hold your head upright, and look straight ahead.

LEFT FORWARD

Step ahead with the left foot.

Bend the knee of your left leg a little, while the right leg in the rear should remain slightly slanting and stretched straight. The toes point outward.

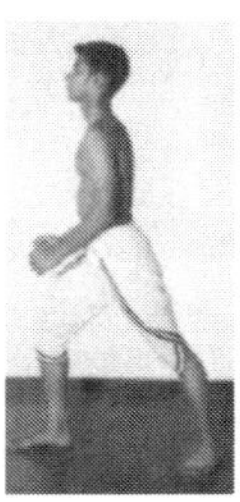

RIGHT FORWARD

Step ahead with the right foot.

Bend the knee of your right leg a little, while the left leg in the rear should remain slanting and stretched straight. The toes point outward.

LONG LEFT FORWARD

Take a long left step forward.

Shift body-weight on to the left leg, bend the knee, and lean body forward. The right leg behind remains straight, the foot pointing to the right side.

As you step forward with the left, thrust both arms forward diagonally, hold them a shoulder width apart, palms facing downward, your fingers held straight.

LONG RIGHT FORWARD

Take a long right step forward.

Shift body-weight on to the right leg, bend the knee, and lean body forward. The left leg behind remains straight, the foot pointing to the left side.

As you step forward with the right, thrust both arms forward diagonally, hold them a shoulder width apart, palms facing downward, your fingers held straight.

PHASES

STRAIGHT RIGHT

- Step forward with the left holding your arms stretched overhead, a shoulder width apart, palms facing outward.
- Swing your right leg high in front, the knee and foot held in a straight line. Aim the swing to touch the right palm with your right foot.
- Bring down the right foot in a single flowing motion, and hold it in line with your left leg.

STRAIGHT LEFT

- Step forward with the right holding your arms stretched overhead, a shoulder width apart, palms facing outward.
- Swing left leg high in front, the knee and foot held in a straight line. Aim the swing to touch the left palm with your left foot.
- Bring down the left foot in a single flowing motion, and hold it in line with your right leg.

OUTWARD RIGHT

- Step left foot forward. Stretch your arms overhead, hold them a shoulder width apart, palms facing outward.
- Swing stretched right leg high, clockwise in front full circle in a single flowing motion. While swinging, brush the right palm with your right foot.
- At the end of the swing, hold it in line with your left leg.

OUTWARD LEFT

- Step right foot forward. Stretch your arms overhead, hold them a shoulder width apart, palms facing outward.
- Swing stretched left leg high, anti-clockwise in front full circle in a single flowing motion. While swinging, brush the left palm with your left foot.
- At the end of the swing, hold it in line with your right leg.

INWARD RIGHT

- Step left foot forward.
- Stretch arms overhead, hold them a shoulder width apart, palms facing outward.
- Swing stretched right leg high, anti-clockwise in front full circle in a single flowing motion. While swinging, brush the right palm with the right foot.
- At the end of the swing, hold it in line with your left leg.

INWARD LEFT

- Step right foot forward.
- Stretch your arms overhead, hold them a shoulder width apart, palms facing outward.
- Swing stretched left leg high, clockwise in front full circle in a single flowing motion. While swinging, brush the left palm with your left foot.
- At the end of the swing, hold it in line with your right leg.

RIGHT TOWARDS LEFT

- Step left foot forward.
- Stretch your arms overhead, hold them a shoulder width apart, palms facing outward.
- Swing stretched right leg high in front, diagonally towards the left. Aim the swing to touch the left palm with your right foot.
- Bring down the right and hold it in line with your left leg.

LEFT TOWARDS RIGHT

- Step right foot forward.
- Stretch your arms overhead, hold them a shoulder width apart, palms facing outward.
- Swing stretched left leg high in front, diagonally towards the right. Aim the swing to touch the right palm with your left foot.
- Bring down the left and hold it in line with your right leg.

SWING RIGHT PIVOTING

- Repeat 'Straight Right'.
- While ending that exercise, pivot by the right and swival to the opposite direction. Then swing your right foot high in front as in 'Straight Right'.
- While ending that, pivot again by the right and swival to the opposite direction. Then swing your right foot high in front as in 'Straight Right'.
  (While pivoting on the left foot, the right foot should not come in contact with the floor except at the end.)

SWING LEFT PIVOTING

- Repeat 'Straight Left'.
- While ending that exercise, pivot by the left and swival to the opposite direction. Then swing your left foot high in front as in 'Straight Left'.
- While ending that, pivot again by the left and swival to the opposite direction. Then swing your left foot high in front as in 'Straight Left'.
  (While pivoting on the right foot, the left foot should not come in contact with the floor except at the end.)

STRAIGHT RIGHT AND SIT

- Repeat 'Straight Right'.
- After ending that exercise, without your right foot touching the floor, place it behind with a long step backwards, and sit on it.
- Your left leg remains stretched straight in front on the floor, the foot stretched and the arc turned to the right.
- Your arms remain straight, palms placed on the floor, on either side of your left thigh.

STRAIGHT LEFT AND SIT

- Repeat 'Straight Left'.
- After ending that exercise, without your left foot touching the floor, place it behind with a long step backwards, and sit on it.
- Your right leg remains stretched straight in front on the floor, the foot stretched and the arc turned to the left.
- Your arms remain straight, palms placed on the floor, on either side of the right thigh.

STRAIGHT RIGHT, SIT, SPRING, TURN AND REPEAT

- Repeat 'Straight Right and Sit'.
- Push the palms downward and spring your body up by straightening your right leg.
- Simultaneously, bend your body slightly towards left and swing it half-circle from left side to right bending backwards in a flowing motion. Keep arms stretched overhead.
- Turning to the opposite direction, sit on the left leg and assume the final posture of 'Straight Left and Sit'.
- Reverse these movements and assume the final posture of 'Straight Right and Sit'.

STRAIGHT LEFT, SIT, SPRING, TURN AND REPEAT

- Repeat 'Straight Left and Sit'.
- Push the palms downward and spring your body up by straightening your left leg.
- Simultaneously, bend your body slightly towards right and swing it half-circle from the right side to the left bending backwards in a flowing motion. Keep arms stretched overhead.
- Turning to the opposite direction, sit on your right leg and assume the final posture of 'Straight Right and Sit'.
- Reverse these movements and assume the final posture of 'Straight Left and Sit'.

SWING BODY HALF CIRCLE

- Stand astride, feet about three-feet apart.
- Bend your body forward, slightly to one side, touch the foot with both palms.
- Then, bending your body backwards, swing it half circle from one side to the other. While doing this, your arms are stretched overhead.
- Bend your body forward and touch the other foot with both palms.
- Thereafter, reverse these movements and complete the exercise by touching the other foot with both palms.

SWING BODY FULL CIRCLE

- Stand astride, feet about three-feet apart.
- Bend your body forward, slightly to one side, touch the foot with both palms.
- Then swing your body full circle, first bending it backwards (half circle) and then bending it forward (half circle). While doing this, your arms are stretched overhead, following the movement of the head.
- Complete the exercise by touching the same foot with the palms.

STRAIGHT RIGHT AND SPLIT

- Repeat 'Straight Right'.
- Continuing the downward motion of your right leg, move it backwards. Slide that leg to sit with a split.
- Your right leg remains stretched behind with the instep on the floor. Your left leg remains stretched straight in front on the floor.
- Your arms remain straight, palms placed on the floor, on either side close to your body.

STRAIGHT LEFT AND SPLIT

- Repeat 'Straight Left'.
- Continuing the downward motion of your left leg, move it backwards. Slide that leg to sit with a split.
- Your left leg remains stretched behind with the instep on the floor. Your right leg remains straight in front on the floor.
- Your arms remain straight, palms placed on the floor, on either side close to your body.

PHASES EXPLAINED

❏ *Done inside a kalari, the practitioner stands at the Eastern end facing the West.*

Phase 1 - BOW AND CROUCH

- Stand upright.
- Move your left foot a shoulder width apart.
- Stretch both arms sideways to shoulder level and palms facing downwards.
- Turn the palms upward and raise your arms overhead and hold palms together.
- Holding the palms together, bring the forearms together vertically in front of your chest.
- Bending your knees apart, lower the trunk between them, parallel to the floor. Hold your shoulders in level with the knees. Hold your head up and look straight.

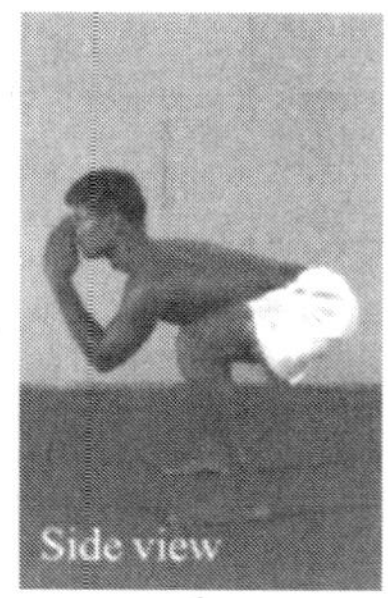
Side view

Phase 2 - STEP LEFT

- In the 'Crouch' posture (Phase 1), step forward with your left foot.
- Unfold the palms, stretch arms down slightly to the front, and hold them a shoulder width apart.
- Your palms remain turned downward, about six inches above the floor.

Phase 3 - SLIDE RIGHT AND STAMP

- After ending Phase 2 move your right foot forward in an arc-wise manner, brushing the instep of the left foot and stamp with it about twelve inches ahead.
- While stepping forward, lift your forearms, hold them vertically and crossed (left in front of the right) in front of your chest.
- While stamping with the right foot, separate your arms and stretch them downward in front, a shoulder width apart, palms facing the floor.

Phase 4 - RETREAT RIGHT

- Withdraw your right foot in an arc-wise manner, by the side of the left instep to stand upright with the right foot in the rear.
- Simultaneously, circle the clenched right hand around your head, the fist moving in line with the left ear and back of the neck.
- Drop the hand on your right side.

Phase 5 - KICK LEFT AND CROUCH

- Kick high in front with the outer edge of your left foot.
- Withdraw that foot to knee level of the supporting right leg. And then slide your left foot to the left, close to the floor.
- Stand astride and 'Bow and Crouch' as in Phase I.

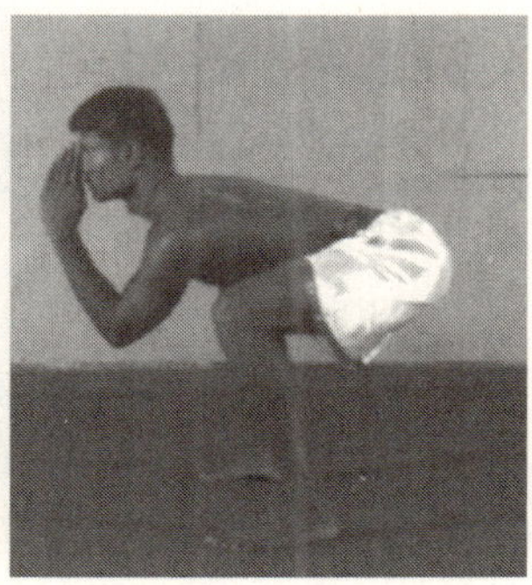

Phase 6 - KICK LEFT, STEP AND LEAP

- Stand upright.
- Kick high in front with the outer edge of your left foot.
- Withdraw that foot to knee level of the supporting right leg.
- Step forward with your left foot.
- Take off on your left foot, leap forward, and land on the right and place your left foot in front.
- While leaping, stretch your arms in front, withdraw them to cross forearms in front of your chest, left in front of the right.
- Assume the 'Crouch' posture, with the left foot ahead, arms still crossed in front of your chest.

Phase 7 - STAMP RIGHT

- Rise from the 'Crouch' posture (at the end of Phase 6).
- Move your right foot forward in an arc-wise manner, brushing the instep of the left foot and stamp ahead.
- Simultaneously, uncross your arms, stretch them down, slightly in front, palms facing the floor.

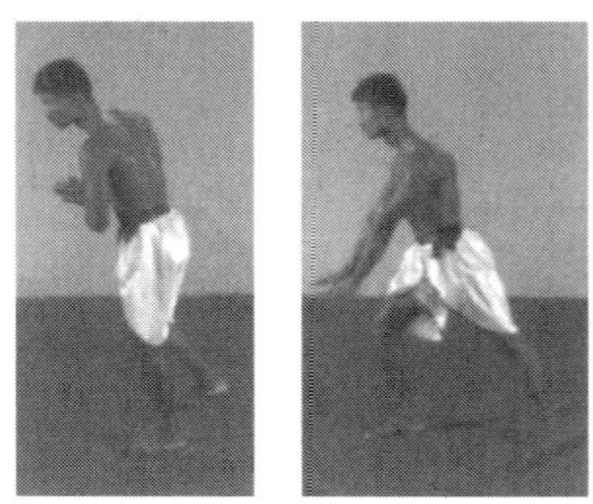

Phase 8 - LUNGE LEFT AND STRETCH

- Take a long left step forward.
- Shift your body-weight on to the left leg, bend the knee, and lean body forward. The right leg behind remains straight, the foot pointing to the right side.
- As you step forward with the left, thrust both arms forward, inclined slightly upward, hold them a shoulder width apart, palms facing downwards, your fingers pointing dioganally upwards.

Phase 9 - STAND UPRIGHT

- Withdraw your left foot, stand astride and upright. The arms are still held stretched overhead.

Phase 10 - STRAIGHT RIGHT

- Step forward with the left holding your arms stretched overhead, a shoulder width apart, palms facing outward.
- Swing your right leg high in front, the knee and foot held in a straight line. Aim the swing to touch the right palm with your right foot.
- Bring down the right foot in a single flowing motion, and hold it in line with your left leg.

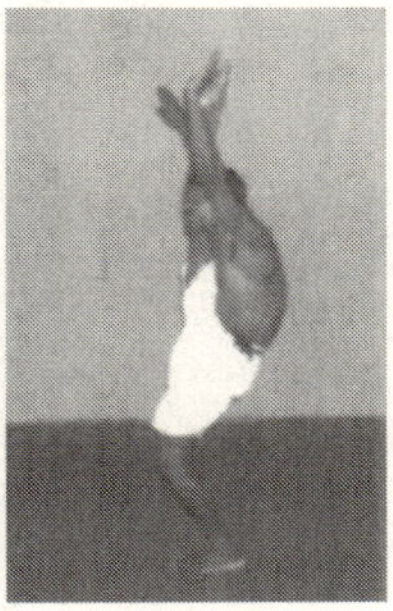

Phase 11 - STRAIGHT LEFT

- Step forward with the right holding your arms stretched overhead, a shoulder width apart, palms facing outward.
- Swing your left leg high in front, the knee and foot held in a straight line. Aim the swing to touch the left palm with your left foot.
- Bring down the left foot in a single flowing motion, and hold it in line with your right leg.

Phase 12 - STRAIGHT RIGHT, KICK LEFT JUMPING, TURN AND LUNGE

- Repeat 'Straight Right' (Phase 10). While ending that Phase, take off by the left foot and execute a high kick in front with it while landing on the right.
- Then pivoting on your right foot, swival by the right to the opposite direction and lunge with a long left stretching your body forward. Shift body-weight on to the left leg, bend the knee, and lean your body forward.
- Your right leg behind remains straight, the foot pointing to the right side. In this position, hold the left forearm inclined to protect your chest, while the right arm is held stretched, to the front.

Phase 13 - STEP LEFT AND CROUCH

- Step left foot forward.
- While stepping forward, rise and stretch your left arm shoulder high in front, palm facing downwards.
- Then, withdraw the left arm towards your body. Hold the forearm inclined to protect your chest.
- Assume the'Crouch' posture.

Phase 14 - TROT

- Remaining in the Crouch posture, with your left foot in front, trot forward and land on your right foot.
- After that trot keep the left foot in front as at the start.
- While trotting, move your left elbow forward as if to jab an opponent in front.

Phase 15 - RETREAT AND JUMP

- Retreat three steps.
- Then, with your right foot in the rear, take off on it, and jump high executing a scissors kick.
- Now move backwards to reach the starting position.

Phase 16 - SWING RIGHT PIVOTING

- Repeat 'Straight Right' (Phase 10).
- While ending that exercise, pivot by the right and swival to the opposite direction. Then swing your right foot high in front as in 'Straight Right'.
- While ending that, pivot again by the right and swival to the opposite direction. Then swing your right foot high in front as in 'Straight Right'.
  (While pivoting on the left foot, the right foot should not come in contact with the floor except at the end.)

Phase 17 - SWING LEFT PIVOTING

- Repeat 'Straight Left' (Phase 11).
- While ending that exercise, pivot by the left and swival to the opposite direction. Then swing your left foot high in front as in 'Straight Left'.
- While ending that, pivot again by the left and swival to the opposite direction. Then swing your left foot high in front as in 'Straight Left'.
  (While pivoting on the right foot, the left foot should not come in contact with the floor except at the end.)

Phase 18 - STRAIGHT RIGHT, TURN AND LUNGE

- Repeat 'Straight Right' (Phase 10).
- While ending that exercise, pivot by the right on your left foot and turn to the opposite direction. Lunge right foot forward with a long step, bend the knee, and lean your body forward.
- Your left leg remains straight behind, the foot pointing to the left side.
- While pivoting, bring the right fist in line with the left ear behind the head. While lunging forward with your right foot, stretch right arm forward.
- Your left forearm remains inclined in front, protecting your chest.

Phase 19 - STRAIGHT RIGHT, TURN AND CROUCH

- Repeat 'Straight Right' (Phase 10).
- While ending that exercise, pivot by the right on your left foot and turn to the opposite direction.
- Stand astride moving your right foot a shoulder width apart.
- Then assume the 'Bow and Crouch' posture (Phase 1).

Phase 20 - RISE, JUMP, LAND AND LUNGE

- Rising from the 'Crouch' posture take off from the left foot and jump up. Before landing on your right foot at the same spot, move your right foot swiftly clockwise at knee level.
- Lift the left foot to be in line with your right knee.
- Turn slightly diagonally to the left and lunge with a long left step.
- While lunging, stretch your right arm in front. Your left forearm remains inclined in front, protecting your chest.

Phase 21 - WITHDRAW BY RIGHT AND TURN

- Withdraw the right arm and hold closed fist in front of your chest.
- Turn by the right to the opposite direction, and take a long forward step with the left foot. Pivot on the left leg, turn your body to the opposite direction by moving your right foot by the rear half circle and keep that leg behind straight with a long step.
- Shift your body-weight on the left leg, bend the knee, and lean your body forward.

Phase 22 - STEP RIGHT, KICK LEFT AND CROUCH

- Move your right foot in an arc-wise manner brushing the instep of the left foot, and step forward.
- Then execute a high kick with your left foot, withdraw it to the level of the right knee, and step forward with your left foot.
- While kicking high with your left foot, stretch the left arm in front and touch the left instep with your outer left palm.
- Bring your palms pressed together in front of your chest, then stretch arms forward at chest level, palms still remaining pressed together.
- Assume the 'Bow and Crouch' posture, but with your left foot in front.

Phase 23 - OUTWARD RIGHT

- Step left foot forward. Stretch your arms overhead, hold them a shoulder width apart, palms facing outward.
- Swing stretched right leg high, clockwise in front full circle in a single flowing motion. While swinging, brush the right palm with your right foot.
- At the end of the swing, hold it in line with your left leg.

Phase 24 - OUTWARD LEFT

- Step right foot forward. Stretch your arms overhead, hold them a shoulder width apart, palms facing outward.
- Swing stretched left leg high, anti-clockwise in front full circle in a single flowing motion. While swinging, brush the left palm with your left foot.
- At the end of the swing, hold it in line with your right leg.

Phase 25 - OUTWARD RIGHT, STEP, TURN, JUMP, KICK AND LUNGE

- Repeat 'Outward Right' (Phase 23).
- Thereafter, step right foot forward.
- Then take off from that foot, turn by the right to the opposite direction, kick high (scissors kick) in front with the right foot, and land on your left foot.
- After the kick, withdraw your foot and keep it behind with a long step backwards.
- Shift your body-weight on to the left leg in front, bend the knee, and lean your body forward.
- Hold the right arm stretched in front. Your left forearm remains guarding your chest.

Phase 26 - INWARD RIGHT

- Step left foot forward.
- Stretch arms overhead, hold them a shoulder width apart, palms facing outward.
- Swing stretched right leg high, anti-clockwise in front full circle in a single flowing motion. While swinging, brush the right palm with the right foot.
- At the end of the swing, hold it in line with your left leg.

Phase 27 - INWARD LEFT

- Step right foot forward.
- Stretch your arms overhead, hold them a shoulder width apart, palms facing outward.
- Swing stretched left leg high, clockwise in front full circle in a single flowing motion. While swinging, brush the left palm with your left foot.
- At the end of the swing, hold it in line with your right leg.

Phase 28 - INWARD RIGHT AND TURN

- Repeat 'Inward Right' (Phase 26).
- While ending that, pivot on your left leg by the left and turn to the opposite direction. Stretch the right leg behind with a long step backwards.
- Shift your body-weight on to the left leg, bend the knee, and lean your body forward.
- Hold your right arm stretched in front. The left forearm remains guarding your chest.

Phase 29 - RIGHT TOWARDS LEFT

- Step left foot forward.
- Stretch your arms overhead, hold them a shoulder width apart, palms facing outward.
- Swing stretched right leg high in front, diagonally towards the left. Aim the swing to touch the left palm with your right foot.
- Bring down the right and hold it in line with your left leg.

Phase 30 - LEFT TOWARDS RIGHT

- Step right foot forward.
- Stretch your arms overhead, hold them a shoulder width apart, palms facing outward.
- Swing stretched left leg high in front, diagonally towards the right. Aim the swing to touch the right palm with your left foot.
- Bring down the left and hold it in line with your right leg.

Phase 31 - STRAIGHT RIGHT AND OUTWARD

- Repeat 'Straight Right' (Phase 10).
- Thereafter, without the right foot touching the floor, repeat 'Outward Right' (Phase 23).

Phase 32 - STRAIGHT LEFT AND OUTWARD

- Repeat 'Straight Left' (Phase 11).
- Thereafter, without the left foot touching the floor, repeat 'Outward Left' (Phase 24).

Phase 33 - STRAIGHT RIGHT, OUTWARD, STRAIGHT

- First repeat 'Straight Right' (Phase 10), then ' Outward Right' (Phase 23) and again repeat 'Straight Right' (Phase 10), all in a flowing motion, without the right foot touching the floor till at the end.

Phase 34 - STRAIGHT LEFT, OUTWARD, STRAIGHT

- First repeat 'Straight Left' (Phase 11), then 'Outward Left' (Phase 24) and again repeat 'Straight Left' (Phase 11), all in a flowing motion, without the left foot touching the floor till at the end.

Phase 35 - STRAIGHT RIGHT, OUTWARD AND PIVOT

- Repeat Phase 10, 23 and 16 all in a flowing motion, without the right foot touching the floor till at the end.

Phase 36 - STRAIGHT RIGHT, OUTWARD, STRAIGHT, OUTWARD

- Repeat Phase 10, 23, 10 and 23 in a flowing motion, without the right foot touching the floor till at the end.

Phase 37 - STRAIGHT LEFT, OUTWARD, STRAIGHT, OUTWARD

- Repeat Phase 11, 24, 11 and 24 in a flowing motion, without the left foot touching the floor till at the end.

Phase 38 - STRAIGHT RIGHT, OUTWARD, STRAIGHT, OUTWARD AND PIVOT

- Repeat Phase 10, 23, 10, 23 and 16 in a flowing motion, without the right foot touching the floor till at the end.

Phase 39 - SWING RIGHT FIVE TIMES

- Repeat Phase 10, 23, 10, 23 and 10 in a flowing motion, without the right foot touching the floor till at the end.

Phase 40 - SWING LEFT FIVE TIMES

- Repeat Phase 11, 24, 11, 24 and again 11 in a flowing motion, without the left foot touching the floor till at the end.

Phase 41 - STRAIGHT RIGHT AND SIT

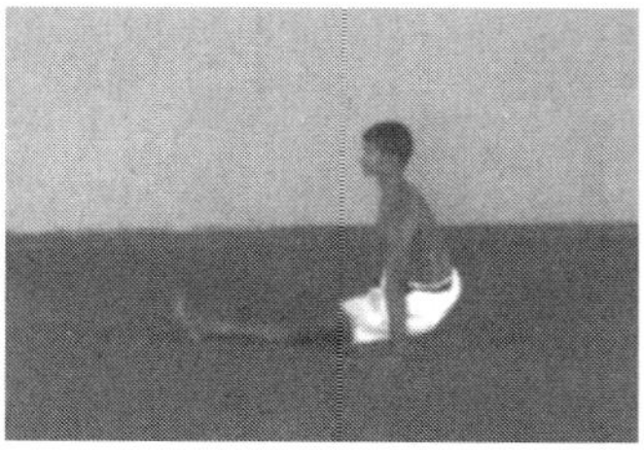

- Repeat 'Straight Right' (Phase 10).
- Thereafter, without your right foot touching the floor, place it behind with a long step backwards, and sit on it.
- Your left leg remains stretched straight in front on the floor, the foot stretched and the arc turned to the right.
- Your arms remain straight, palms placed on the floor, on either side of your left thigh.

Phase 42 - STRAIGHT LEFT AND SIT

- Repeat 'Straight Left' (Phase 11).
- Thereafter, without your left foot touching the floor, place it behind with a long step backwards, and sit on it.
- Your right leg remains stretched straight in front on the floor, the foot stretched and the arc turned to the left.
- Your arms remain straight, palms placed on the floor, on either side of the right thigh.

Phase 43 - STRAIGHT RIGHT, SIT, SPRING, TURN AND REPEAT

- Repeat 'Straight Right and Sit' (Phase 41).
- Push the palms downward and spring your body up by straightening your right leg.
- Simultaneously, bend your body slightly towards left and swing it half-circle from left side to right bending backwards in a flowing motion. Keep arms stretched overhead.
- Turning to the opposite direction, sit on the left leg and assume the final posture of Phase 42.
- Reverse these movements and assume the final posture of Phase 41.

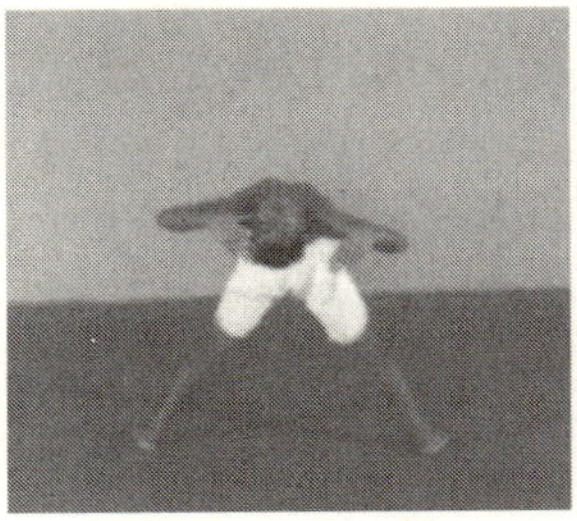

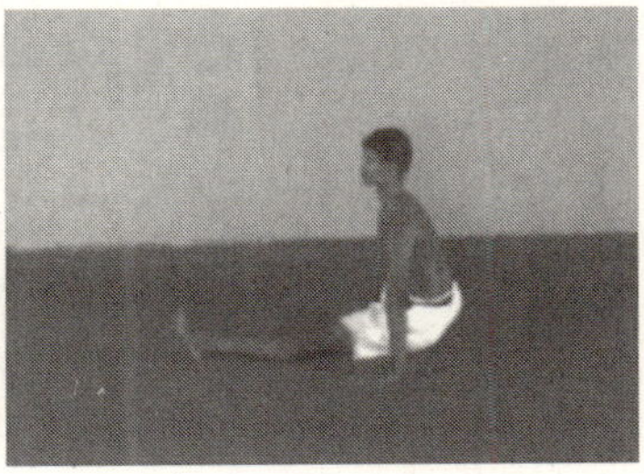

Phase 44 - STRAIGHT LEFT, SIT, SPRING, TURN AND REPEAT

- Repeat 'Straight Left and Sit' (Phase 42).
- Push the palms downward and spring your body up by straightening your left leg.
- Simultaneously, bend your body slightly towards right and swing it half-circle from the right side to the left bending backwards in a flowing motion. Keep arms stretched overhead.
- Turning to the opposite direction, sit on your right leg and assume the final posture of Phase 41.
- Reverse these movements and assume the final posture of Phase 42.

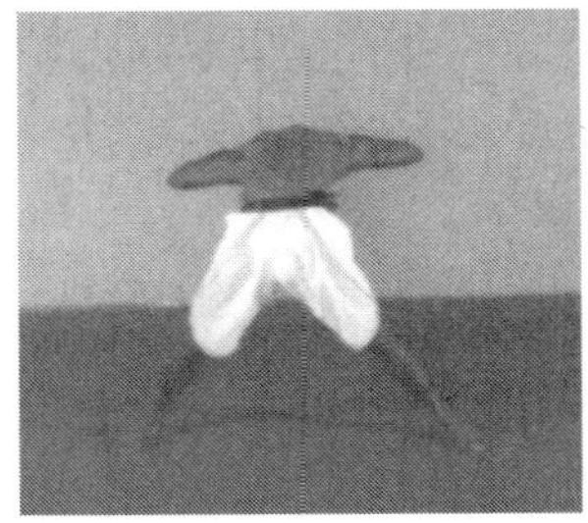

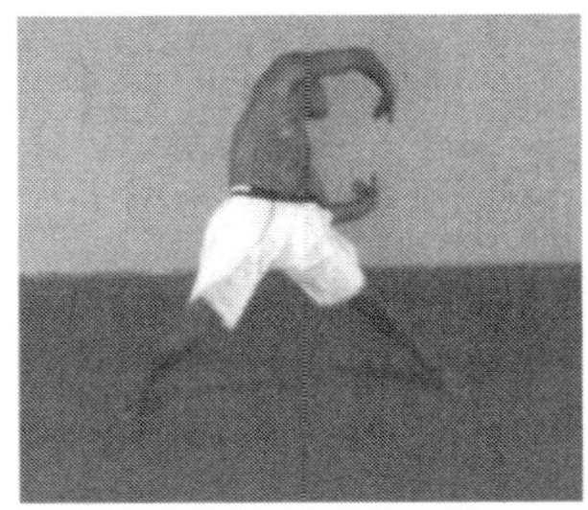

Phase 45 - SWING BODY HALF CIRCLE

- Stand astride, feet about three-feet apart.
- Bend your body forward, slightly to one side, touch the foot with both palms.
- Then, bending your body backwards, swing it half circle from one side to the other. While doing this, your arms are stretched overhead.
- Bend your body forward and touch the other foot with both palms.
- Thereafter, reverse these movements and complete the exercise by touching the other foot with both palms.

Phase 46 - SWING BODY FULL CIRCLE

- Stand astride, feet about three-feet apart.
- Bend your body forward, slightly to one side, touch the foot with both palms.
- Then swing your body full circle, first bending it backwards (half circle) and then bending it forward (half circle). While doing this, your arms are stretched overhead, following the movement of the head.
- End this Phase by touching the same foot with the palms.

Phase 47 - STRAIGHT RIGHT AND SIT, SPRING, TURN AND REPEAT; SWING BODY HALF CIRCLE

- Repeat Phase 43.
- Thereafter, get up by moving the right foot forward to bring it in line with the left foot and in a flowing motion, move it about three feet towards your right to stand astride.
- Then repeat Phase 45, starting from the left side.

Phase 48 - STRAIGHT LEFT AND SIT, SPRING, TURN AND REPEAT; SWING BODY HALF CIRCLE

- Repeat Phase 44.
- Thereafter, get up by moving your left foot forward to bring it in line with the right foot and in a flowing motion, move it about three feet towards your left to stand astride.
- Then repeat Phase 45, starting from the right side.

Phase 49 - STRAIGHT RIGHT AND SIT, SPRING, TURN AND REPEAT; SWING BODY FULL CIRCLE

- Repeat Phase 43.
- Thereafter, get up by moving your right foot forward to bring it in line with the left foot and in a flowing motion, move it about three feet towards your right to stand astride.
- Then repeat Phase 46, starting from the left side, twice in succession.

Phase 50 - STRAIGHT LEFT AND SIT, SPRING, TURN AND REPEAT; SWING BODY FULL CIRCLE

- Repeat Phase 44.
- Thereafter, get up by moving your left foot forward to bring it in line with the right foot and in a flowing motion, move it about three feet towards your left to stand astride.
- Then repeat Phase 46, starting from the right side, twice in succession.

Phase 51 - STRAIGHT RIGHT AND SPLIT

- Repeat 'Straight Right' (Phase 10).
- Continuing the downward motion of your right leg, move it backwards. Slide that leg to sit with a split.
- Your right leg remains stretched behind with the instep on the floor. Your left leg remains stretched straight in front on the floor.
- Your arms remain straight, palms placed on the floor, on either side close to your body.

Phase 52 - STRAIGHT LEFT AND SPLIT

- Repeat 'Straight Left' (Phase 11).
- Continuing the downward motion of your left leg, move it backwards. Slide that leg to sit with a split.
- Your left leg remains stretched behind with the instep on the floor Your right leg remains straight in front on the floor Your arms remain straight, palms placed on the floor, on either side close to your body.

Phase 53 - TURN AND STRAIGHT LEFT

- Turn by the right to the opposite direction, and repeat 'Straight Left' (Phase 11).

Phase 54 - TURN AND STRAIGHT RIGHT

- Turn by the left to the opposite direction, and repeat 'Straight Right' (Phase 10).

Phase 55 - SLIDE RIGHT AND STEP LEFT

- Stand with a long left step forward, the knee bent, and your body-weight on the left leg.
- Slide your right foot forward, brushing the instep of the left foot, in an arc-wise manner and keep it in front.
- Then step forward with your left foot.

Phase 56 - SLIDE RIGHT, SCISSORS KICK AND SQUAT

- Slide your right foot forward, brushing the instep of your left foot, in an arc-wise manner.
- Stamp right foot in front.
- Spring high on it and execute a scissors kick.
- Land on your left foot and assume the 'Squat' posture. (In the 'Squat' posture, keep your right leg folded behind the body, the knee touching the floor in front, a little towards the right. Sit balancing on the toes, the heel of your right foot vertically up.)

Phase 57 - BOW DUCKING, STRAIGHTEN BODY AND RETREAT

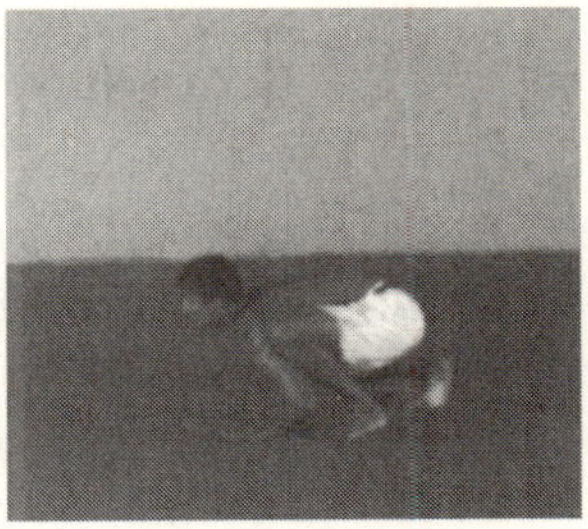

- Remaining in the 'Squat' posture, place your palms in front, on the floor, a shoulder width apart. Bow, stretch your body forward, bring the chest down almost to touch the floor.
- Push up, straighten your body while still in the 'Squat' posture.
- Then stand upright with the left foot in front.
- Retreat a few steps.

Phase 58 - RETREAT, PIVOT, KICK HIGH AND SIT

- Retreat a few steps.
- With your right foot in the rear, pivot a full circle, clockwise on it. Take off on the right foot while pivoting and execute a scissors kick with it.
- After landing on your left foot, sit back on your right foot, that foot in the rear as explained in Phase 41.

Phase 59 - STAND ASTRIDE AND SPRING

- Rise up by moving your right foot forward and bring it in line with the left foot. In a flowing motion, slide it towards the right and stand astride.
- Then spring up on both your feet, and execute a high kick in front with your right foot.
- Then land on your left foot.

Phase 60 - (TURN) RIGHT TOWARDS LEFT

- Turn by the left to the opposite direction.
- Repeat Phase 29.

Phase 61 - (TURN) LEFT TOWARDS RIGHT

- Turn by the right to the opposite direction.
- Repeat Phase 30.

Phase 62 - OUTWARD RIGHT, TURN, INWARD LEFT, TURN

- Repeat Phase 23, simultaneously turning to the opposite direction by the right.
- Standing on your right foot, repeat Phase 27, simultaneously turning again by the right to assume the original position.

Phase 63 - INWARD RIGHT, TURN FULL CIRCLE AND SIT BACK

- Repeat Phase 26.
- Simultaneously, pivot by the left full circle on your left foot and sit back with the right foot in the rear as in Phase 41.

Phase 64 - TURN FULL CIRCLE BENDING BACKWARDS

- Stand upright and astride, feet a shoulder width apart.
- Step right foot diagonally forward to the left. Lean your body forward a little. Cross forearms (right outside the left) in front of your chest.
- Turn by the left, on the left foot, and assume the original position as at the start of this Phase. While turning, bend your body backwards.

Phase 65 - BOW AND STRETCH

- With a long left step in front, stretch your body forward.
- Hold the folded arms in front of your chest, with the forearms vertically together.

Phase 66 - STEP RIGHT AND TOUCH FLOOR

- With a long right step in front, stretch your body forward.
- Touch the floor with the right finger tips in reverence.

Phase 67 - TOUCH LEFT INSTEP

- Without stepping right repeat 'Kick left and Crouch' of Phase 22.

Phase 68 - BOW DUCKING, STRAIGHTEN BODY

- Repeat 'Bow Ducking, Straighten Body' of Phase 57.

Phase 69 - RISE UP AND TURN

- Rise and stand upright from the 'Squat' posture.
- Move your right foot, clockwise, through the rear and turn to the opposite direction. Keep your right foot behind.

Phase 70 - STAMP RIGHT AND PROTECT

- Slide your right foot forward, brushing the instep of the left foot, and stamp ahead.
- While doing this, cross forearms and then stretch the right arm in front at chest level as if delivering a punch, clenched fist turned upwards. Your left arm remains guarding your chest.

Phase 71 - POUNCE ON RIGHT AND TOUCH FLOOR

- Pounce into the *kalari* with your right foot in front, and facing the *poothara* touch the floor with your right hand finger tips in reverence.

Phase 72 - STEP RIGHT AND LEFT

- Step forward with the right and then with the left.

Phase 73 - PROTECT AND BOW

- Remain in the 'Squat' posture.
- Cross arms in front of your chest, right over the left, and touch both the knees, the left knee with the right and right knee with the left.
- Uncross the arms, bring them up to shoulder level, stretched sideways, with palms facing upwards.
- Then fold arms and touch shoulders with the fingers.
- Bring the palms pressed together in front of your chest, stretch arms forward at chest level. Fold arms and hold them in front of the chest with the forearms vertically together.
- Bend your body backwards, the folded arms still held close to the chest.
- Bring body forward and straighten it, the folded arms still in position. (See Phase 41 of 'Short Staff' and Phase 87 of 'Otta' for identical movements)

ORAL COMMANDS

First Salutation

Bow and Stretch (Phase 65), Step right and Touch floor (Phase 66), Touch Left Instep (Phase 67), Bow ducking, Straighten body (Phase 68), Touch Left Instep (Phase 67), Rise up and Turn (Phase 69), Step right, Kick left and Crouch (Phase 22), Rise up and Turn (Phase 69), Step right, Kick left and Crouch (Phase 22), Bow ducking, Straighten body (Phase 68), Touch Left Instep (Phase 67), Stamp right and Protect (Phase 70), Withdraw by right and Turn (Phase 21), Step right, Kick left and Crouch (Phase 22)

(While starting the salutation in a traditional *kalari*, stand facing the *poothara*, about ten feet from it.)

Second Salutation

(This veneration is done only as a prelude to an actual duel)

Pounce on right and Touch floor (Phase 71), Retreat right (Phase 4), Kick left, Step left and Leap (Phase 6), Stamp right (Phase 7), Retreat right (Phase 4), Touch Left Instep (Phase 67), Outward right (Phase 23), Step left and Crouch (Phase 13), Trot (Phase 14), Stamp right (Phase 7), Retreat right (Phase 4), Touch Left Instep (Phase 67), Bow ducking, Straighten body (Phase 68), Rise up and Turn (Phase 69), Step right and left (Phase 72), Rise up and Turn (Phase 69), Step right, Kick left and Crouch (Phase 22), Protect and Bow (Phase 73)—Here repeat the hand movements thrice—Bow ducking, Straighten body (Phase 68), Touch Left Instep (Phase 67), Step right and Protect (Phase 70), Withdraw by right and Turn (Phase 21), Step right, Kick high and Crouch (Phase 22)

First Series

A. Bow and Crouch (Phase 1), Step Left (Phase 2), Slide Right and Stamp (3), Retreat Right (4), Kick Left and Crouch (5), Step Left (2), Slide Right and Stamp (3), Retreat Right (4)

B. Kick Left, Step and Leap (6), Slide Right and Stamp (3), Lunge Left and Stretch (8), Stand Upright (9), Straight Right (10), Straight Left (11), Straight Right, Kick Left Jumping, Turn and Lunge (12)

C. *Repeat B and reach the starting point.*

D. Kick Left, Step and Leap (6), Slide Right and Stamp (3), Step Left and Crouch (13), Trot (14), Stamp Right (7), Retreat and Jump (15)

E. Kick Left, Step and Leap (6), Slide Right and Stamp (3), Lunge Left and Stretch (8), Stand Upright (9), Swing Right Pivoting (16), Swing Left Pivoting (17), Straight Right, Turn and Lunge (18).

F. *Repeat E and reach the starting point.*

G. *Repeat D.*

H. Kick Left, Step and Leap (6), Slide Right and Stamp (3), Lunge Left and Stretch (8), Stand Upright (9), Straight Right (10), Straight Left (11), Straight Right, Turn and Crouch (19)

I. *Repeat 'H' and reach the starting point.*

J. *Repeat D.*

K. Kick Left, Step and Leap (6), Stamp Right (7), Step Left and Crouch (13), Trot (14), Rise, Jump, Land and Lunge (20), Withdraw by right and turn (21), Step Right, Kick Left and Crouch (22).

Second Series

A. *Repeat A of First Series.*

B. Kick Left, Step and Leap (6), Slide Right and Stamp (3), Lunge Left and Stretch (8), Stand Upright (9), Outward Right (23), Outward Left (24), Outward Right, Step, Turn, Jump, Kick and Lunge (25).

C. *Repeat B and reach the starting point.*

D. *Repeat D of First Series.*

E. Kick Left, Step and Leap (6), Slide Right and Stamp (3), Lunge Left and Stretch (8), Stand Upright (9), Inward Right (26), Inward Left (27), Inward Right and Turn (28).

F. *Repeat E and reach the starting point.*

G. *Repeat D of First Series.*

H. Kick Left, Step and Leap (6), Slide Right and Stamp (3), Lunge Left and Stretch (8), Stand Upright (9), Right towards Left (29), Left towards Right (30), Inward Right and Turn (***28***).

I. *Repeat H and reach the starting point.*

J. *Repeat D of First Series.*

K. *Repeat K of First Series.*

Third Series

A. *Repeat A of First Series.*

B. Kick Left, Step and Leap (6), Slide Right and Stamp (3), Lunge Left and Stretch (8), Stand Upright (9), Straight Right and Outward (31), Straight Left and Outward (32), Straight Right and Outward (31), Straight Left (11), Straight Right, Kick Left Jumping, Turn and Lunge (12).

C. *Repeat B and reach the starting point.*

D. *Repeat D of First Series.*

E. Kick Left, Step and Leap (6), Slide Right and Stamp (3), Lunge Left and Stretch (8), Stand Upright (9), Straight Right, Outward, Straight (33), Straight Left, Outward, Straight (34), Straight Right, Outward and Pivot (35), Swing Left pivoting (17), Straight Right, Turn and Lunge (18).

F. *Repeat E and reach the starting point.*

G. *Repeat D of First Series.*

H. *Repeat K of First Series.*

Fourth Series

A. *Repeat A of First Series.*

B. Kick Left, Step and Leap (6), Slide Right and Stamp (3), Lunge Left and Stretch (8), Stand Upright (9), Straight Right, Outward, Straight (33), Straight Left, Outward, Straight (34), Straight Right, Outward, Straight (33), Straight Left (11), Straight Right, Kick Left Jumping, Turn and Lunge (12).

C. *Repeat B and reach the starting point.*

D. *Repeat D of First Series.*

E. Kick Left, Step and Leap (6), Slide Right and Stamp (3), Lunge Left and Stretch (8), Stand Upright (9), Straight Right, Outward, Straight, Outward (36), Straight Left, Outward, Straight, Outward (37), Straight Right, Outward, Straight, Outward and Pivot (38), Swing Left pivoting (17), Straight Right, Turn and Lunge (18).

F. *Repeat E and reach the starting point.*

G. *Repeat D of First Series.*

H. *Repeat K of First Series.*

Fifth Series

A. *Repeat A of First Series.*

B. Kick Left, Step and Leap (6), Slide Right and Stamp (3), Lunge Left and Stretch (8), Stand Upright (9), Swing Right five times (39), Straight Left (11), Swing Right five times (39),

Straight Left (11), Straight Right, Kick Left jumping, Turn and Lunge (12).

C. *Repeat B and reach the starting point.*

D. *Repeat D of First Series.*

E. Kick Left, Step and Leap (6), Slide Right and Stamp (3), Lunge Left and Stretch (8), Stand Upright (9), Straight Right (10), Swing Left five times (40), Straight Right (10), Swing Left five times (40), Swing Right pivoting (16), Swing Left pivoting (17), Straight Right, Turn and Lunge (18).

F. *Repeat E and reach the starting point.*

G. *Repeat D of First Series.*

H. *Repeat K of First Series.*

Sixth Series

A. *Repeat A of First Series.*

B. Kick Left, Step and Leap (6), Slide Right and Stamp (3), Lunge Left and Stretch (8), Stand Upright (9), Straight Right and Sit (41), Straight Left and Sit (42), Straight Right and Sit (41), Straight Left (11), Straight Right, Kick Left jumping, Turn and Lunge (12).

C. *Repeat B and reach the starting point.*

D. *Repeat D of First Series.*

E. Kick Left, Step and Leap (6), Slide Right and Stamp (3), Lunge Left and Stretch (8), Stand Upright (9), Straight Right, Sit, Spring, Turn and Repeat (43), Straight Left, Sit, Spring, Turn and Repeat (44), Straight Right, Sit, Spring, Turn and Repeat (43), Swing Right pivoting (16), Swing Left pivoting (17), Straight Right, Turn and Lunge (18).

F. *Repeat E and reach the starting point.*

G. *Repeat D of First Series.*

H. *Repeat K of First Series.*

Seventh Series

A. *Repeat A of First Series.*

B. Kick Left, Step and Leap (6), Slide Right and Stamp (3), Lunge Left and Stretch (8), Stand Upright (9), Straight Right and Sit, Spring, Turn and Repeat; Swing body half circle (47), Straight Left and Sit, Spring, Turn and Repeat; Swing body half circle (48), Straight Right and Sit, Spring, Turn and Repeat; Swing body half circle (47), Swing Right pivoting (16), Swing Left pivoting (17), Straight Right, Turn and Lunge (18).

C. *Repeat B and reach the starting point.*

D. *Repeat D of First Series.*

E. *Repeat K of First Series.*

Eighth Series

A. *Repeat A of First Series.*

B. Kick Left, Step and Leap (6), Slide Right and Stamp (3), Lunge Left and Stretch (8), Stand Upright (9), Straight Right and Sit, Spring, Turn and Repeat; Swing body full circle (49), Straight Left and Sit, Spring, Turn and Repeat; Swing body full circle (50), Straight Right and Sit, Spring, Turn and Repeat; Swing body full circle (49), Swing Right pivoting (16), Swing Left pivoting (17), Straight Right, Turn and Lunge (18).

C. *Repeat B and reach the starting point.*

D. *Repeat D of First Series.*

E. *Repeat K of First Series.*

Ninth Series

A. *Repeat A of First Series.*

B. Kick Left, Step and Leap (6), Slide Right and Stamp (3), Lunge Left and Stretch (8), Stand Upright (9), Straight Right (10), Turn and Straight Left (53), Turn and Straight Right (54), Straight

Left (11), Turn and Straight Right (54), Turn and Straight Left (53), Straight Right (10), Retreat and Jump (15), Slide Right and Step Left (55), Straight Right, Kick Left jumping, Turn and Lunge (12), Slide Right, Scissors Kick and Squat (56), Bow ducking, Straighten body and Retreat (57).

C. *Repeat B and reach the starting point.*

D. Kick Left, Step and Leap (6), Slide Right and Stamp (3), Step Left and Crouch (13), Trot (14), Stamp Right (7), Retreat, Pivot, Kick high and Sit (58), Straight Right, Sit, Spring, Turn and repeat (43 without 41), Stand Astride and Spring (59).

E. *Repeat K of First Series.*

Tenth Series

A. *Repeat A of First Series.*

B. Kick Left, Step and Leap (6), Slide Right and Stamp (3), Lunge Left and Stretch (8), Stand Upright (9), Straight Right (10), Straight Left (11), Straight Right (10), Turn and Straight Left (53), Straight Right (10), Straight Left (11), Turn and Straight Right (54), Straight Left (11), Turn and Straight Right (54), Straight Left (11), Straight Right (10), Turn and Straight Left (53), Straight Right (10), Retreat and Jump (15), Slide Right and Step Left (55), Straight Right, Kick Left jumping, Turn and Lunge (12), Slide Right, Scissors Kick and Squat (56), Bow ducking, Straighten body and Retreat (57).

C. *Repeat B and reach the starting point.*

D. Kick Left, Step and Leap (6), Slide Right and Stamp (3), Step Left and Crouch (13), Trot (14), Stamp Right (7), Retreat, Pivot, Kick high and Sit (58), Straight Right, Sit, Spring, Turn and repeat (43 without 41), Swing body half circle (45), Stand Astride and Spring (59).

E. *Repeat K of First Series.*

Eleventh Series

A. *Repeat A of First Series.*

B. Kick Left, Step and Leap (6), Slide Right and Stamp (3), Lunge Left and Stretch (8), Stand Upright (9), Right towards Left (29), Left towards Right (30), (Turn) Right towards Left (60), Left towards Right (30), Turn and Straight Right (54), Retreat and Jump (15), Slide Right and Step Left (55), Straight Right, Kick Left jumping, Turn and Lunge (12), Slide Right, Scissors Kick and Squat (56), Bow ducking, Straighten body and Retreat (57).

C. *Repeat B and reach the starting point.*

D. Kick Left, Step and Leap (6), Slide Right and Stamp (3), Step Left and Crouch (13), Trot (14), Stamp Right (7), Retreat, Pivot, Kick high and Sit (58), Straight Right, Sit, Spring, Turn and repeat (43 without 41), Swing body half circle (45), Swing body full circle (46), Stand Astride and Spring (59).

E. *Repeat K of First Series.*

Twelfth Series

A. *Repeat A of First Series.*

B. Kick Left, Step and Leap (6), Slide Right and Stamp (3), Lunge Left and Stretch (8), Stand Upright (9), Right towards Left (29), plus Outward Right (23), Left towards Right (30) plus Outward Left (24), (Turn) Right towards Left (60) plus Outward Right (23), Left towards Right (30) plus Outward Left (24), Turn and Straight Right (54), Retreat and Jump (15), Slide Right and Step Left (55), Straight Right, Kick Left jumping, Turn and Lunge (12), Slide Right, Scissors Kick and Squat (56), Bow ducking, Straighten Body and Retreat (57).

C. *Repeat B and reach the starting point.*

D. *Repeat, D of Eleventh Series.*

E. *Repeat K of First Series.*

Thirteenth Series

A. *Repeat A of First Series.*

B. Kick Left, Step and Leap (6), Slide Right and Stamp (3), Lunge Left and Stretch (8), Stand Upright (9), Outward Right, Turn, Inward Left, Turn (62), Straight Right (10), Turn and Straight Left (53), Turn and Straight Right (54), Retreat and Jump (15), Slide Right and Step Left (55), Straight Right, Kick Left jumping, Turn and Lunge (12), Slide Right, Scissors Kick and Squat (56), Bow Ducking, Straighten Body and Retreat (57).

C. *Repeat B and reach the starting point.*

D. *Repeat D of Eleventh Series.*

E. *Repeat K of First Series.*

Fourteenth Series

A. *Repeat A of First Series.*

B. Kick Left, Step and Leap (6), Slide Right and Stamp (3), Lunge Left and Stretch (8), Stand Upright (9), Outward Right, Turn, Inward Left, Turn (62), Inward Right, Turn full circle and Sit Back (63), Outward Right *plus* Right towards Left (29), Outward Left (24) *plus* Left towards Right (30), (Turn), Outward Right (23) *plus* Right towards Left (29), Outward Left (24) *plus* Left towards Right (30), Turn and Straight Right (54), Retreat and Jump (15), Slide Right and Step Left (55), Straight Right, Kick Left jumping, Turn and Lunge (12), Slide Right, Scissors Kick and Squat (56), Bow ducking, Straighten Body and Retreat (57).

C. *Repeat B and reach the starting point.*

D. Kick Left, Step and Leap (6), Slide Right and Stamp (3), Step Left and Crouch (13), Trot (14), Stamp Right (7), Retreat, Pivot, Kick High and Sit (58), Straight Right, Sit, Spring, Turn and Repeat (43 without 41), Inward Right, Turn full circle and Sit Back (63), Turn full circle bending backwards (64), Stand Astride and Spring (59).

E. *Repeat K of First Series.*

EXERCISES WITH WOODEN WEAPONS
(*Kolethaarippayattu*)

Kolethaarippayattu contains a series of exercises with wooden weapons of different lengths and shapes. There are various techniques employed in defending and attacking with them.

The exercises in *kolethaari* also help as foundationals for wielding sharp weapons in *payattu.*

In *kolethaari* one learns to wield *pandeeran*, defend and attack with *kettukaari*, *muchaan* and *otta.*

Exercises with the *pandeeran* (a five-foot long cane or bamboo staff) are done without a sparring partner while exercises with the *kettukaari* (a staff similar to *pandeeraan*), *muchaan* (short-staff) and *otta* (the double curved, horn-shaped baton) are done in pairs.

In *kolethaari* as in *maippayattu*, the Series begins with simple exercises and systematically and gradually goes on to the more complex, difficult and powerful ones.

Swinging the Long Staff
(*Pandeeraan Veeshal*)

Pandeeraan veeshal is a part of *kolethaari*. The swinging exercises are done with a cane or bamboo staff which is generally five or five-and-a-half feet long and about three inches in circumference.

Swinging the *pandeeraan* is excellent for developing suppleness of one's wrist and speed of movement. To start with, each exercise may be done slowly and carefully. Once the practitioner has mastered the swinging movements, and the footwork, the exercises could be done in quick succession.

In all these, done without a sparring partner, the attacks are aimed at imaginary opponents. However, the rapidly swinging *pandeeraan* can be effectively employed in actual defence and attack.

Pandeeraan veeshal shows striking similarity to *silambam* of Tamil Nadu and *bana* of Central India.

Learn each exercise by swinging the staff and moving the feet slowly to perfect the movements. As you gain confidence, start swinging the staff faster without breaking the flow while stepping forward, backwards, turning and jumping. As you swing the staff faster, your movements will resemble a forceful series of attacks, the swinging staff producing a continuous hum.

There are no specific groupings of exercises to form a Series. The staff may be swung starting with Phase 1 and going on through to Phase 19 without breaking the flow of the staff. Or the staff may be swung, any one Phase blending with any other, without adhering to the chronological sequence given to the Phases. In any case, ensure that the swings form an unbroken chain.

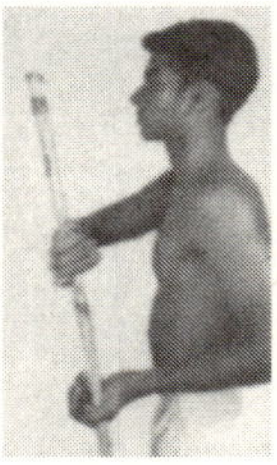

Fig. 1 gripping the long staff

PHASES EXPLAINED

Phase I - HIT HEAD

- Stand with the left foot in front, your body leaning slightly forward.
- Grip the staff as in Fig. I, and hold it vertically at chest level, on your left side, the hit-end of the staff pointing the floor.
- Swing the staff clockwise from your left side, then anti-clockwise from your right side in a vertical plane aiming to hit on the head of the imaginary opponent in front of you.
- One swing follows the next without breaking the flow of the staff
- You may repeat these movements a few times.

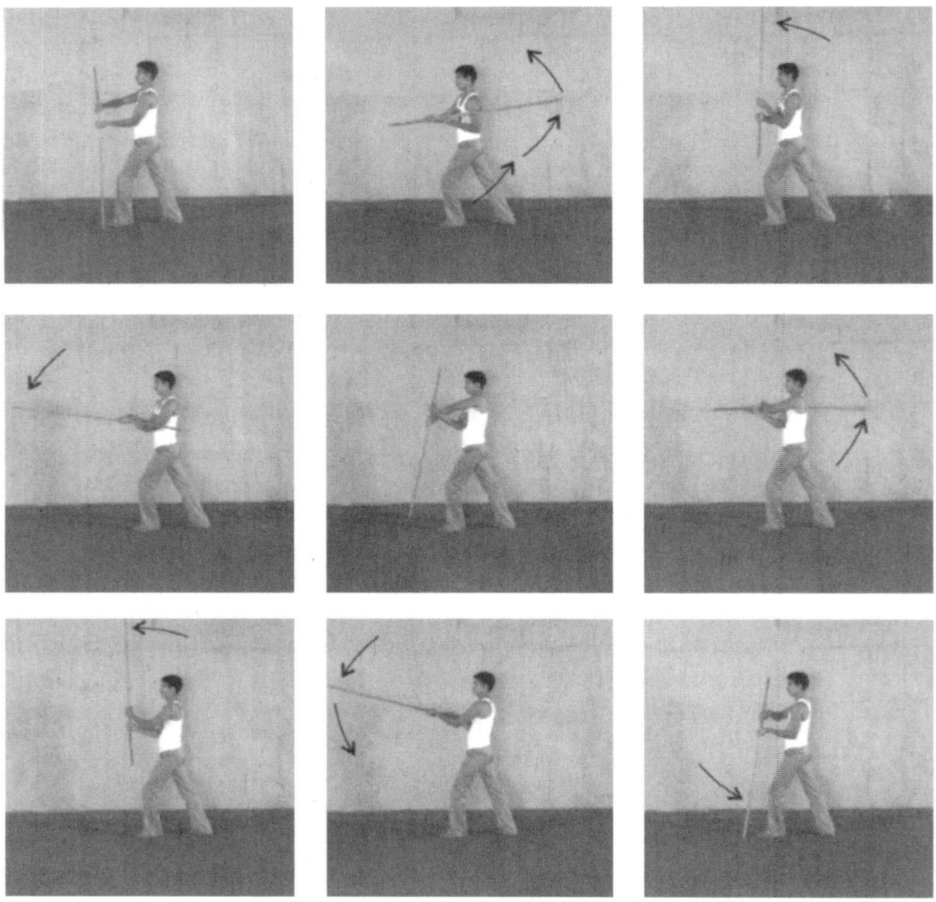

Phase 2 - HIT CHIN

- Stand with the left foot in front, your body leaning slightly forward.
- Grip the staff as in Fig. I, and hold it vertically at chest level, on your left side, the hit end of the staff resting on the floor.
- Swing the staff upwards in an anticlockwise manner from your left side, then clockwise from your left side in a vertical plane, aiming to hit at the chin of the imaginary opponent in front of you.
- The first upward swing follows the next without breaking the flow of the staff.
- You may repeat these movements a few times.

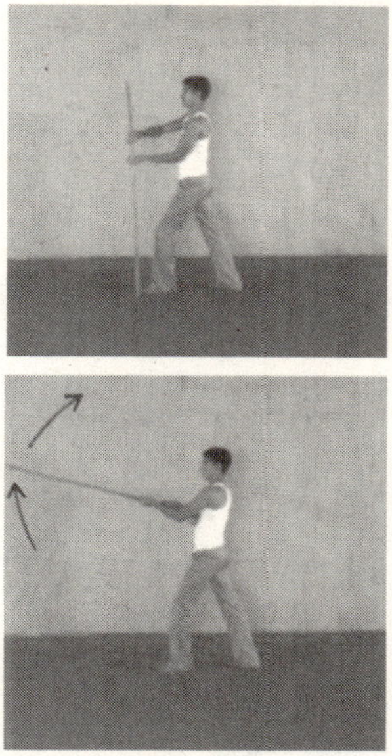

Phase 3 - HIT HEAD AND CHIN TURNING ON LEFT

- Repeat Phase I.
- When the staff comes to the left side of your body, and when the hit-end of the staff points the floor, step forward with your right foot and then turn by the left to the opposite direction.
- Now swing the staff clockwise in a vertical plane on your right side, and then repeat Phase 2, with your left foot in front.

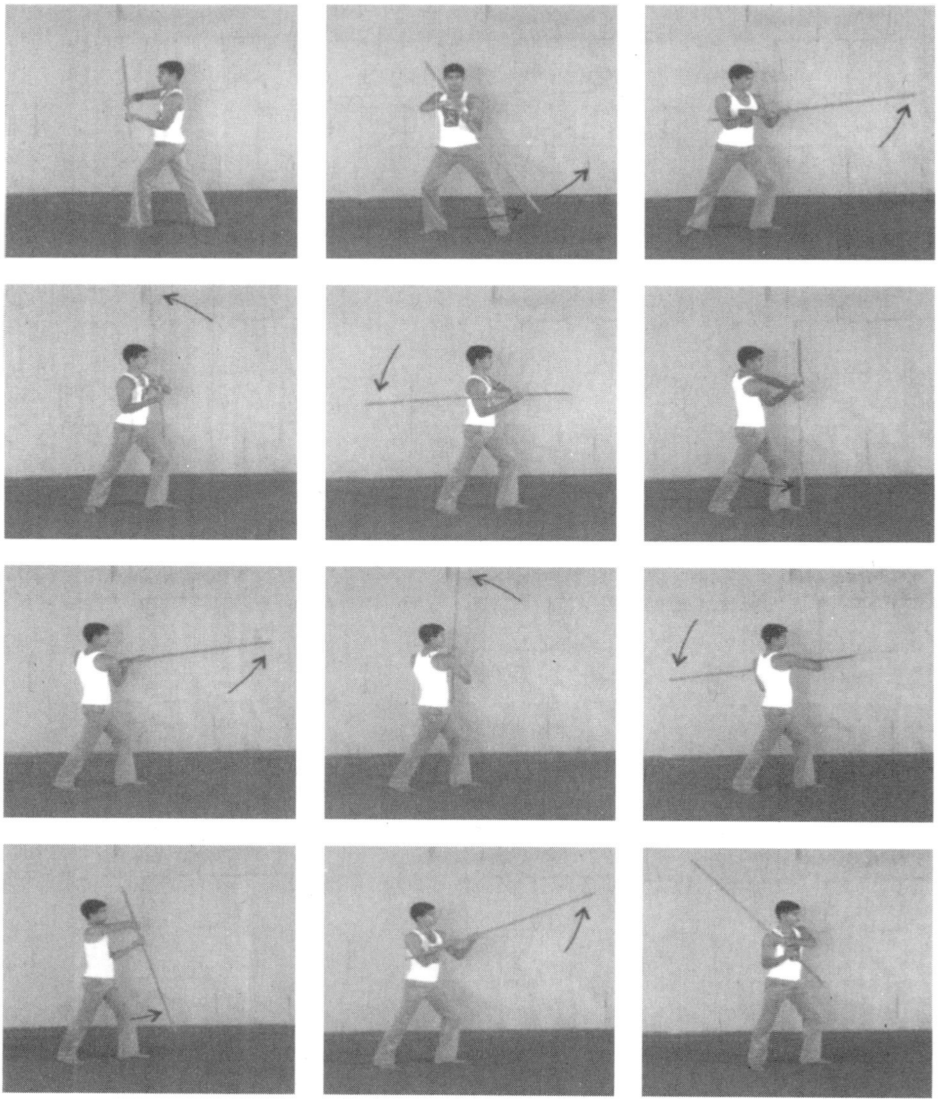

- Without breaking the flow of the staff, and when the staff moves upwards on your right side, step forward with your right foot and then turn by the left to the opposite direction.
- Repeat Phase I, with your left foot in front.

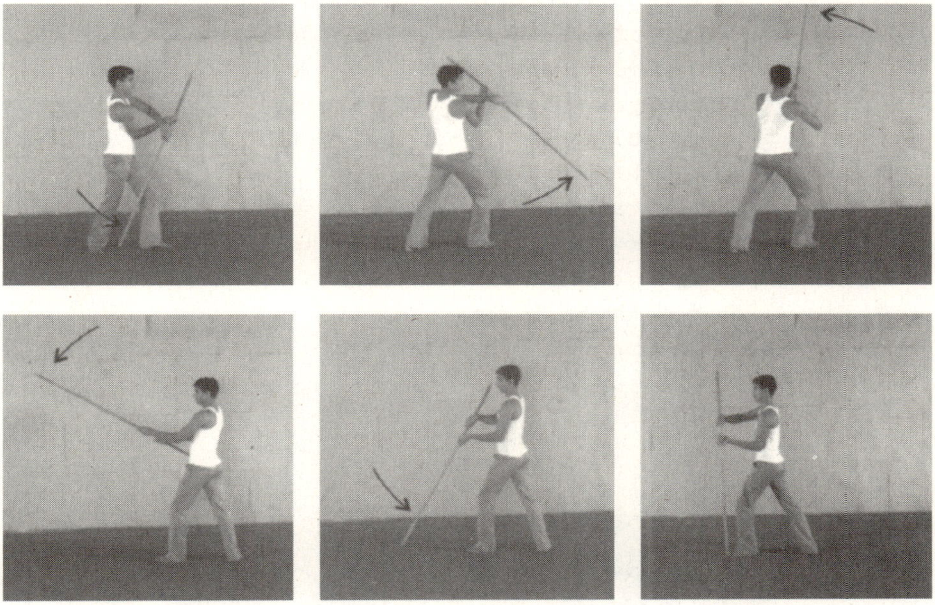

Phase 4 - HIT HEAD AND CHIN TURNING ON RIGHT

- Repeat Phase I.
- When the staff comes to the right side of your body, and when the hit-end of the staff points the floor, turn by the right to the opposite direction, and then step forward with your left foot.
- Now swing the staff anti-clockwise in a vertical plane on your left side, and then repeat Phase 2, with your left foot in front.
- Without breaking the flow of the staff, and when the staff moves upwards on your left side, turn by the right to the opposite direction and then step forward with your left foot.
- Repeat Phase I, with your left foot in front.

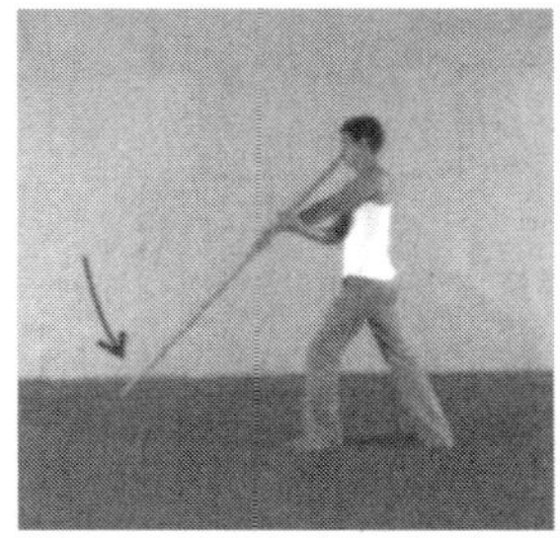

Phase 5 - HIT HEAD AND CHIN STEPPING FORWARD

- Stand with the left foot in front, your body leaning slightly forward.
- Hold the staff vertically, the hit-end pointing upwards, on your right side slightly in front. The grip on the staff should be near the right side of your chest. Stepping forward with the right foot, hit on the opponent's head.
- Allow the staff to move downward towards the left, and then turn to the opposite direction by the left. While turning, swing the staff clockwise in a vertical plane on your right side and hit the opponent's chin with the left foot in front.
- Without breaking the flow of the staff, and when the staff moves upwards on your left side, turn to the opposite direction by the right, and then stepping forward with the left foot, hit the opponent on his head.
- Allow the staff to move downward towards the right, and when the hit-end of the staff comes pointed on to the floor on your right side, turn to the opposite direction by the right, swing the staff anti-clockwise in a vertical plane on your left side and hit the opponent's chin with the right foot in front.
- Without breaking the flow of the staff, continue the upward swing from the right side of your body, turn to the opposite direction by the left and step forward with the right foot and then hit the opponent on his head.

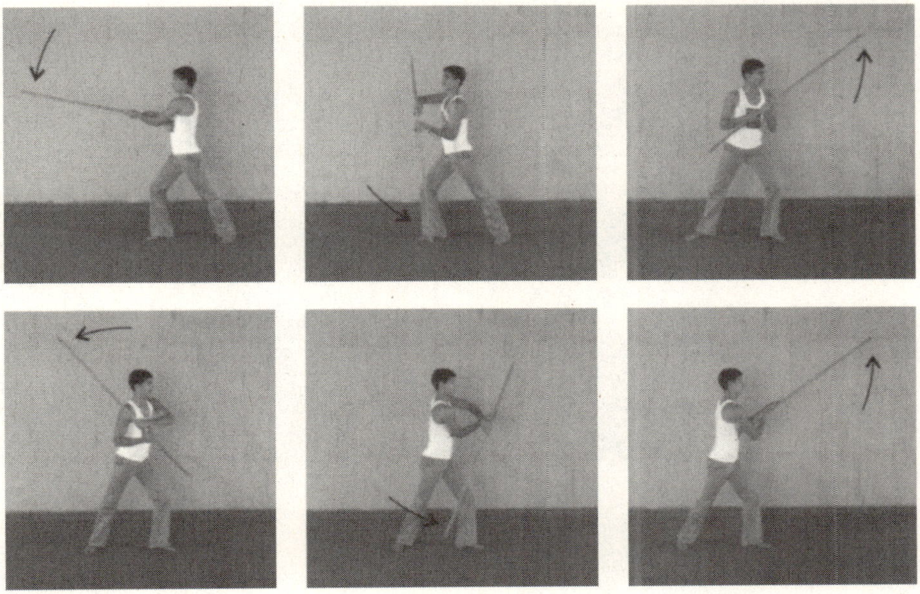

Phase 6 - HIT HEAD AND CHIN STEPPING BACKWARDS

- Hold the staff as in Phase 5.
- Aim a hit on the head of the opponent in front. And while the staff moves downward towards the left, step back your left foot and turn by the left to the opposite direction. Now swing the staff vertically and clockwise on your right side and aim a hit at the opponent's chin.
- Continue swinging it vertically in an anti-clockwise manner from the left side aiming at the chin. Then turn to the opposite direction by the right. And without breaking the flow of the staff, aim a hit on the head.
- Continue the movement of the staff downward to the right, hit-end pointing to the floor, step back with your right foot and turn to the opposite direction by the right and swing the staff vertically in an anti-clockwise manner on the left side hitting the chin.
- Continue the movement of the staff and while it moves upwards from the right, turn to the opposite direction by the left and step back with your left foot hitting the head.

Phase 7 - HIT HEAD AND CHIN TURNING (FORWARD)

- Hold the staff as in Phase 5 . Step forward with the right and hit on the opponent's head. Continue the movement of the staff downward on the left side of your body, and turn to the opposite direction by the left. Then continue to swing the staff clockwise vertically on the right side of your body and hit the opponent's chin. Without breaking the flow of the staff, turn by the left to the opposite direction, and hit on the opponent's head while stepping forward with your left foot.
- Repeat Phase I.

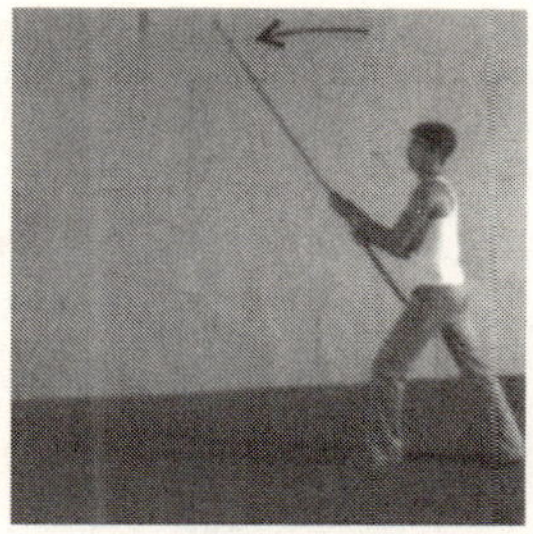

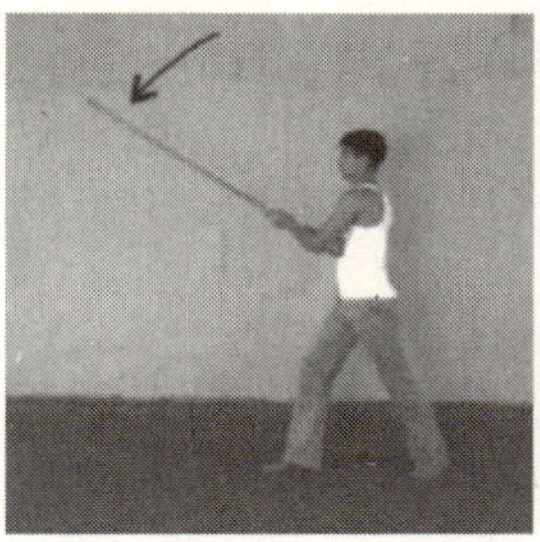

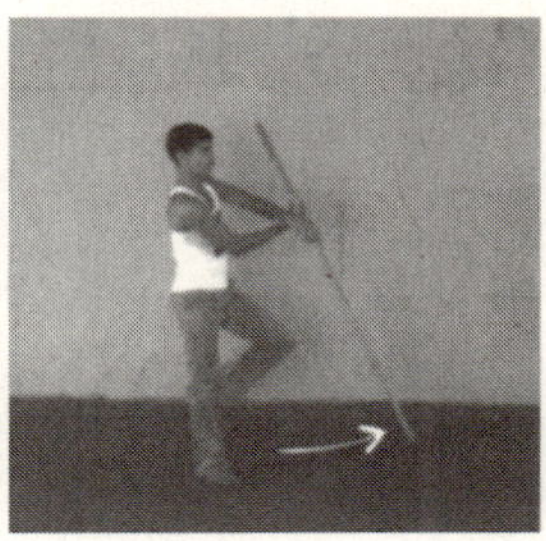

Phase 8 - HIT HEAD AND CHIN TURNING (BACKWARDS)

- Repeat Phase I.
- When the staff moves downwards from the left to your right, turn to the opposite direction by the right. Swing staff vertically anti-clockwise on your left and hit the opponent's chin.
- Then step forward with the left foot, turn to the opposite direction by your right, and hit the opponent's head while stepping your right foot backwards.
- Repeat Phase I.

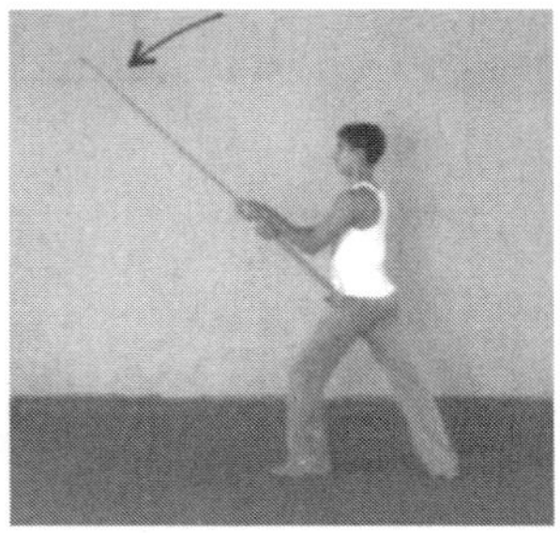

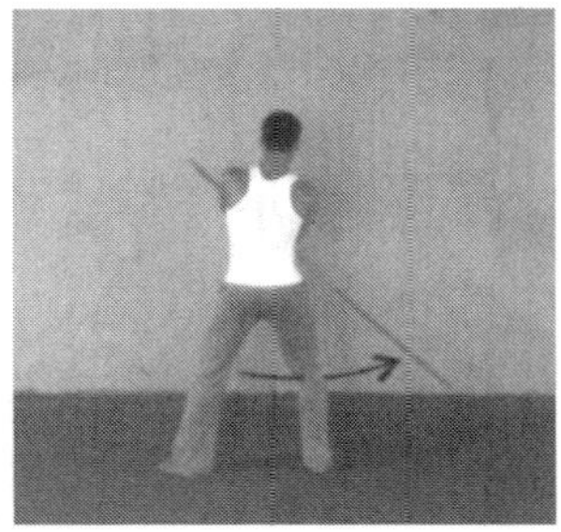

Phase 9 - HIT HEAD AND CHIN JUMPING AND TURNING (FORWARD)

- Repeat Phase 7.
- But instead of stepping forward by the right, jump by the right and hit on the opponent's head, and continue doing all the other movements of Phase 7.

Phase 10 - HIT HEAD AND CHIN JUMPING AND TURNING (BACKWARDS)

- Repeat Phase 8.
- But instead of stepping forward with your left foot and turning to the opposite direction, jump on the left foot and turn to the opposite direction and hit on the opponent's chin. Thereafter, continue doing all the other movements of Phase 8.

Phase 11 - HIT HEAD BENDING LEFT (FORWARD) - UNDERARM

- Repeat Phase I.
- After the staff has moved anti-clockwise on your right side and come vertically, the hit-end pointing upwards, continue moving the staff downward, till it reaches vertically on the right side itself, the hit-end pointing downward. Bend your body a little to the left.
- Loosen the left-hand-grip on the staff a little. Lift your right elbow a little to allow the smooth flow of the staff under your right arm, and continue to swing the staff in an anti-clockwise manner, the left palm moving by the side of your right armpit, hit the head of the opponent in front by stepping forward with your right foot.

Phase 12 - HIT HEAD BENDING RIGHT (FORWARD) - UNDERARM

- After Phase 11, without breaking the flow of the staff, swing it clockwise on the left side of your body, and bring it vertically, the hit-end pointing upwards.
- Change your right-hand-grip to be about six inches above the left-grip the palm of the right facing outward. Bend your body a little to the right. Then lifting your left elbow a little to allow the smooth flow of the staff under your left arm, swing the staff downward clockwise, the right grip passing by the side of your left armpit. Hit the head of the opponent in front by stepping forward with your left foot.
- (While doing these - Phase 11 and 12 - in succession, alternate the gripping position of your right hand.)

Phase 13 - HIT HEAD BENDING LEFT (RETREATING) - UNDERARM

- Repeat Phase I.
- Step your left foot backwards, hit on the head of the opponent swinging the staff from your right side as explained in Phase 11.

Phase 14 - HIT HEAD BENDING RIGHT (RETREATING) - UNDERARM

- After ending Phase 13, step your right foot backwards while hitting on the head of the opponent swinging the staff from your left side as explained in Phase 12.

Phase 15 - HIT HEAD BENDING LEFT (TURNING AND ADVANCING)

- Repeat Phase 11.
- Turn to the opposite direction by the left, swing the staff clockwise in a vertical plane on your right side, and hit the opponent's chin.
- Turn to the opposite direction by the left, step forward with your left foot, and hit on the opponent's head.
- Repeat Phase I.

Phase 16 - HIT HEAD BENDING RIGHT (TURNING AND RETREATING)

- Repeat Phase 14.
- Turn to the opposite direction by the right, change the right-hand grip as in Fig. I, swing the staff anti-clockwise in a vertical plane on your left side and hit at the chin of the opponent by taking a step forward with your left foot.
- Then, without breaking the flow of the staff, turn to the opposite direction by the right, and hit the opponent on his head while stepping backwards with your right foot.
- Repeat Phase I.

Phase 17 - HIT HEAD BENDING LEFT (JUMPING, TURNING AND ADVANCING)

- Repeat Phase 11.
- But instead of hitting the opponent's head by stepping forward, hit the head by jumping forward on your right foot.
- Thereafter, continue the movement of the staff and feet as in Phase 15.

Phase 18 - HIT HEAD BENDING RIGHT (JUMPING, TURNING AND RETREATING)

- Repeat Phase 16.
- But instead of hitting the opponent's chin by stepping forward, hit his chin by jumping forward on your left foot.

Phase 19 - COMBINATION

- With your left foot in front, repeat Phase I.
- Without breaking the flow of your staff, continue to repeat several Phases like Phase 1, 2, 3,4, II, 12, and so on.
- While doing these, your left foot in front should remain there almost unchanged, while your right foot in the rear may be slowly moved in an anti-clockwise manner to go full circle.
- However, while aiming hits at the opponent's chin or turning around, your left foot may be lifted and moved, but thereafter, bring it forward to the original position.
- The swinging staff should move smoothly and without breaking the flow from the start to the finish. When one full circle is completed, close the swing of the staff by tucking it under your right armpit, the hit-end of the staff pointing backwards.
- Each exercise may be repeated several times. Take care to proceed from one Phase to the other by weaving the swing without breaking the flowing motion of the staff. You may interchange the series of Phases as is convenient, without rigidly following the sequential order given to these Phases in the 'Phases Explained' notes.

Exercises with the Long Staff (*Kettukaarippayattu*)

The *kettukaari* staff is identical to the one used for *pandeeraan veeshal.*

There are techniques to attack (aimed at the head, chin, temples, torso, ribs and legs) and techniques to defend such attacks.

These are foundationals for the more advanced and complex techniques using other weapons.

The exercises in *kettukaarippayattu* are practised in pairs. One takes on the master's (M) role, while the other takes on the pupil's (P) role.

Grip end ▷ 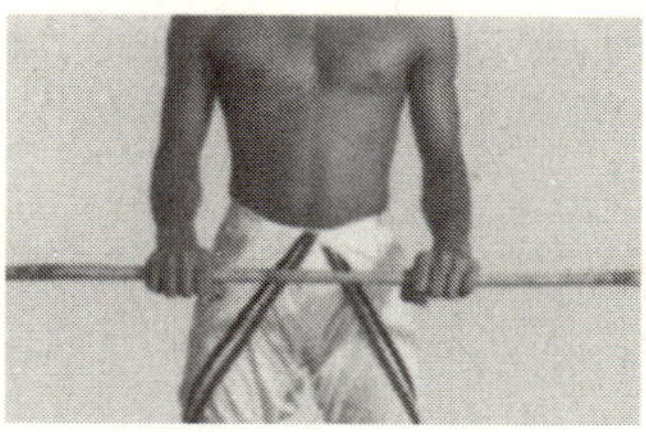 ◁ ***Hit end***

Fig. 1 gripping the long staff

Fig. 2 gripping the long staff

PHASES EXPLAINED

- ❑ *Done inside a kalari, M and P stand in the West and East in the middle of the kalari facing each other while starting these exercises.*
- ❑ *Slide your grips one after the other to either half of staff, as is appropriate, to make room for defence and attack.*
- ❑ *The male in white tracksuit is M; the female in black and white is P.*

Phase 1 - STEP RIGHT AND THRUST

Action P

- Hold staff as in Fig. I. Stand with your left foot in front slightly leaning forward.
- Step forward with the right and thrust at M's chest with the tip of the hit-end.

Action M

- Hold the staff as in Fig. I. Stand with your left foot in front slightly leaning forward.
- Step back with the left and ward off the thrust by swinging the hit-end of the staff from the left to the right.

Phase 2- RETREAT AND WARD OFF THRUST

Action P

- Step back your right foot and ward off M's thrust on the chest by moving the hit-end of the staff from the left to right.

Action M

- Step forward with the left and thrust the tip of the hit-end at P's chest.

Phase 3 - STEP RIGHT AND HIT ANKLE

Action P

- Hold staff as in Fig. 2. Swing staff clockwise overhead, step forward with your right and hit aiming at M's inner right ankle with the hit-end.

Action M

- Hold staff as in Fig. 2. Swing the staff in the same manner as P and defend hit at the right inner ankle with the hit-end by stepping your left foot backwards.

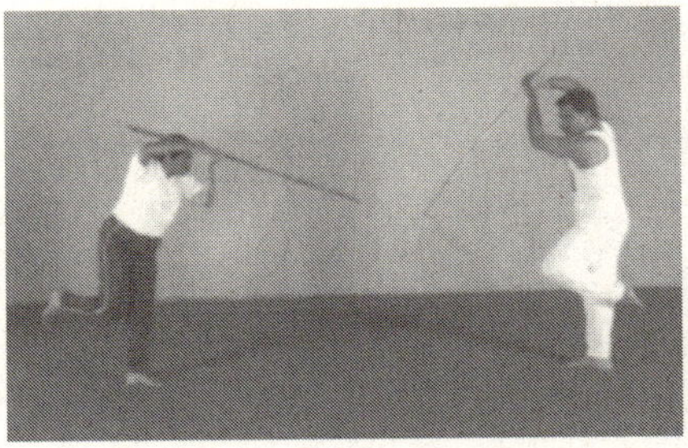

Phase 4 - RETREAT RIGHT AND DEFEND ANKLE

Action P

- Swing the staff from the right to left overhead in an anti-clockwise manner. Stepping right foot backwards, defend M's hit on the left inner ankle with the hit-end.

Action M

- Swing the staff from the right to left overhead in an anti-clockwise manner. Stepping forward with the left, aim a hit at P's inner left ankle, with the hit-end.

Phase 5 - CROSS HIT ENDS

Action P and M

- Hold the staff as in Fig. I. Standing with the left foot in front P and M face each other, and cross the staff at chest level. Here the hit-end of your staff remains close to the opponent's right temple.

Phase 6 - HIT LEFT AND RIGHT TEMPLES AND LEFT ANKLE

Action P

- Step forward with the right and hit aiming at M's left temple with the grip-end.
- Then step forward with the left and hit aiming at M's right temple with the hit-end.
- Remaining in the same position, swing the hit-end of the staff downward in an arc-wise manner and hit at the inner left ankle of M with the hit-end.

Action M

- Step backwards with the left and defend P's hit aimed at the left temple with the grip-end, swinging the staff in the same manner as P.
- Then step back with the right foot and defend P's hit at the right temple with the hit-end.
- Remaining in the same position, swing the hit-end of the staff downward in an arc-wise manner and defend P's hit at the inner left ankle.

Phase 7 - DEFEND THRUST, RETREAT LEFT, DEFEND TEMPLE, RETREAT RIGHT, DEFEND TEMPLE, DEFEND ANKLE AND SWIRL

Action P

- Step backwards with your left foot, defend M's thrust by warding off the staff with the hit-end, moving it from the left to right.
- Standing with the right foot in front, defend hit on the left temple with the grip-end of the staff by moving it from the right to left.
- Then stepping back with the right foot, defend hit on the right temple with the hit-end of the staff by moving it from the left to right.
- Remaining in the same position, defend hit at the inner left ankle with the hit-end by moving the staff downward in an arc-wise manner.
- Then crouch and scoop up M's staff with the hit-end and swirl it to the left side and press.

Action M

- Stepping forward with your right foot, aim a thrust at P's chest with the hit-end of the staff.
- Remaining in the same position with the right foot forward, hit at P's left temple with the grip-end of the staff by moving it from right to left.
- Stepping forward with the left foot, hit at P's right temple with the hit-end of the staff by moving it from the left to right.
- Remaining in the same position, hit at P's left inner ankle with the hit-end by swinging the staff downwards in an arc-wise manner.
- Now M's staff gets scooped up and swirled.

Phase 8 - STEP RIGHT AND HIT THREE

Action P

- Step right foot forward. Hit aiming at M's left temple, then right inner ankle and again left temple by moving the grip-end from top to bottom and back upwards in rapid succession.

Action M

- Step back left foot. Defend the three hits aimed at left temple, right inner ankle and again left temple with the grip-end, moving the staff the same way as P.

Phase 9 - STEP LEFT AND HIT THREE

Action P

- Step left foot forward. Hit aiming at M's right temple, then left inner ankle and again right temple by moving the hit-end from top to bottom and back upwards in rapid succession.

Action M

- Step back right foot. Defend the three hits aimed at right temple, left inner ankle and again right temple with the hit-end moving the staff the same way as P.

Phase 10 - HIT TEMPLE AND ANKLE

Action P

- Stepping forward with the left, hit at M's right temple with the hit-end of the staff. Remaining in the same position, hit also at M's left inner ankle.

Action M

- Stepping backwards with the right defend P's hit aimed at the right temple, and left inner ankle with the hit-end of the staff moving the staff as P.

Phase 11 - STEP BACK LEFT AND DEFEND THREE HITS

Action P

- Step back left foot. Defend hits at left temple, right inner ankle and again left temple with the grip-end of the staff.

Action M

- Step forward with the right. Hit P's left temple, right inner ankle and again left temple with the grip-end of the staff.

Phase 12 - STEP BACK RIGHT AND DEFEND THREE HITS

Action P

- Step back right foot. Defend hits at right temple, left inner ankle and again right temple with the hit-end of the staff.

Action M

- Step forward left foot. Hit P's right temple, left inner ankle and again right temple with the hit-end of the staff.

Phase 13 - STEP RIGHT AND HIT HEAD

Action P

- Step right forward and hit at M's head by moving the grip-end of the staff from your right side in an anti-clockwise manner.

Action M

- Step left foot backwards, ward off P's hit aimed at the head with the grip-end by moving the staff from the right to left, in front above.

Phase 14 - STEP LEFT AND HIT ANKLE

Action P

- Step forward with the left foot and aim hit with the hit-end at M's left inner ankle by moving the staff slanting down to right.

Action M

- Step right foot backwards and defend hit with the hit-end by moving the staff in the same manner as P.

Phase 15 - HIT FOUR AND CIRCLE

Action P and M

- Stepping forward slightly to the left with the right foot, hit with the grip-end at M's left temple.
- Then stepping forward with the left foot, aim a hit at M's right temple with the hit-end, then moving the right foot slightly towards the left in the rear and facing each other directly, aim a hit at M's left inner ankle with the hit-end. Remaining in the same position, lift the hit-end and aim again a hit at M's right temple.
- M defends all these hits repeating the foot and staff movements as P.
- Repeat four or five times these four hits and defence moving in a full circle clockwise till both P and M come to the starting position.

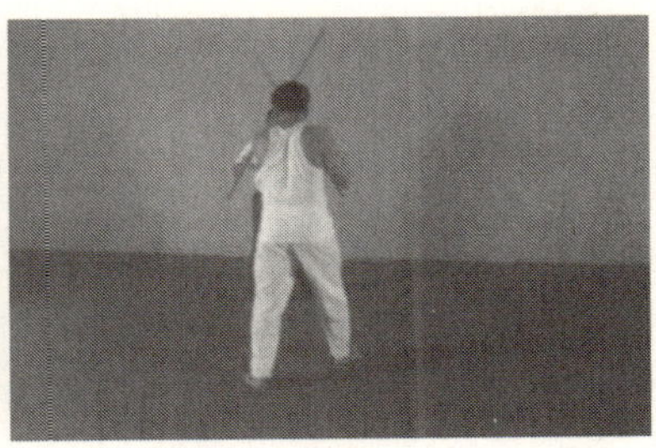

Phase 16 - LUNGE RIGHT AND DEFEND LEFT RIBS

Action P

- Stepping forward slightly to the left with a long right step, defend M's hit aimed at the left ribs by stretching arms forward slightly to the left. The staff should be held vertically with the hit-end pointing upwards. Receive the hit in the middle of the staff, between the grips.

Action M

- Hold the staff as in Fig. 2. Stepping forward with a long right step, aim a hit at P's left ribs with the hit-end of the staff, swinging the staff overhead in a clockwise manner.

Phase 17 - RETREAT RIGHT AND DEFEND RIGHT RIBS

Action P

- Turn the staff anti-clockwise in front of the body to bring the hit-end pointing downward. Step back right foot and thrust staff slightly to the right to defend hit aimed at the right ribs. Receive the hit in the middle of the staff, between the grips.

Action M

- Hold the staff as in Fig. 2. Stepping forward with the left, swing it overhead anti-clockwise from the right to left and hit at P's right ribs.

Phase 25 - STEP RIGHT AND PUSH

Action P

- Gripping the staff as in Fig. I, step forward with the right and push M with a thrust of the staff. While doing this, the staff should be held slanting in front of the chest with the hit-end pointing upwards slightly to the left.

Action M

- Step back left foot and defend P's thrust with a counter thrust, holding the staff in the same manner as P.

Phase 26 - STEP LEFT AND PUSH

Action P

- Gripping the staff as in Fig. I, step forward with the left and push M with a thrust of the staff. While doing this, the staff should be held slanting in front of the chest with the grip-end pointing upwards slightly to the right.

Action M

- Step back right foot and defend P's thrust with a counter thrust, holding the staff in the same manner as P.

Phase 27 - RETREAT RIGHT AND PUSH

Action P

- Gripping the staff as in Fig. I, retreat right foot and push the staff forward. While doing this the staff should be held slanting in front of the chest, grip-end pointing upwards slightly to the right.

Action M

- Step left foot forward and execute a counter push holding the staff in the same manner as P.

Phase 28 - RETREAT LEFT AND PUSH

Action P

- Gripping the staff as in Fig. I, retreat left foot and push the staff forward. While doing this the staff should be held slanting in front of the chest, the hit-end pointing upwards slightly to the left.

Action M

- Step forward with the right foot and execute a counter push holding the staff in the same manner as P.

Phase 29 - HIT LEFT AND RIGHT TEMPLES AND INNER AND OUTER ANKLES

Action P

- Hold staff as in Fig. 2. Step towards the left diagonally slightly to the front with the right foot, and hit with the hit-end aiming at M's left temple.
- Again step forward with the left foot and hit with the hit-end aiming at M's right temple.
- Moving the right foot slightly to the left, in the rear, face M directly and execute a hit at M's left inner ankle with the hit-end, and remaining in the same position swing the staff overhead in a clockwise manner and hit aiming at M's left outer ankle.

Action M

- M continues all movements as P and defends all hits.
- (Rotating clockwise, P and M repeat these exercises four or five times and complete full circle, and assume the original position.)

Phase 30 - DEFEND RIBS, HEAD AND CHEST CIRCLING

Action P

- Hold the staff as in Fig. I. Stepping forward slightly to the left with a long right step, defend M's hit aimed at the left ribs by stretching arms forward slightly to the left. While doing this, the staff should be held vertically in front with the hit-end pointing upwards.
- Then step forward with the left foot and defend hit on the right ribs by thrusting the staff forward and receiving the hit in the middle of the staff. While doing this, the staff should be turned upside down, anti-clockwise and held vertically in front slightly to the right with the grip-end pointing upwards.
- Then move right foot slightly to the left in the rear, face each other directly and defend M's hit aimed at the head. While defending, push up the staff overhead and keep it horizontally, grip-end turned to the right to receive the hit in the middle of the staff.
- Remaining in the same position, push down the staff and defend thrust at the middle of the chest.
- Remaining in the same position, again defend hit at the head by pushing the staff overhead.

Action M

- Grip the staff as in Fig. 2. Stepping forward slightly to the left with a long right step hit at P's left ribs with the hit-end of the staff, by swinging it around the head in a clockwise manner.
- Then step forward with the left foot and hit at P's right ribs swinging the staff around the head in an anti-clockwise manner.
- Moving the right foot in the rear, slightly to the left, face each other directly and hit at P's head with the hit-end of the staff.
- Swing back the staff vertically by the right side clockwise and execute a thrust aimed at P's chest.
- Remaining in the same position, swing the staff by the right side anti-clockwise and execute a hit at P's head.

  (Rotating clockwise, P and M repeat these exercises four or five times and complete full circle, and assume the original position.)

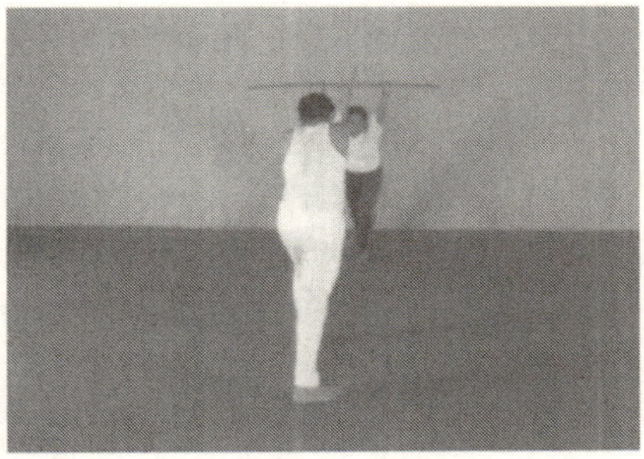

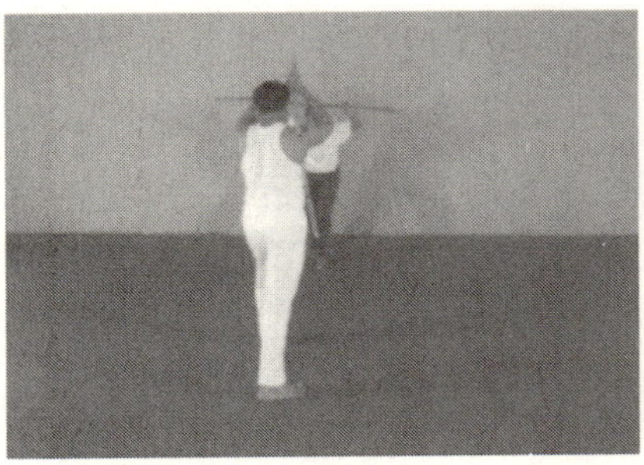

Phase 31 - HIT ANKLE, TEMPLES, ANKLE AND HIT PIVOTING

Action P

- Hold the staff as in Fig. 2, and step right foot forward swinging the staff overhead in a clockwise manner, hit M's right inner ankle.
- Remaining in the same position, hit at M's left temple with the hit-end.
- Stepping back with the right foot, aim a hit at M's right temple with the hit-end.
- Remaining in the same position, execute a hit at M's left inner ankle with the hit-end of the staff.
- Stepping forward with the right foot and changing the grip of the staff (as in Fig. I) execute a hit at M's left temple with the grip-end of the staff.
- Pivot on the left foot by the left and turn full circle and stand facing M, right foot in the rear. While pivoting, change the grip as in Fig. 2 and hit at M's left outer ankle with the hit-end of the staff.
- Remaining in the same position, left foot in front, hit at M's right temple with the hit-end of the staff.

Action M

- Hold the staff as in Fig. 2, and step right foot forward and swing the staff overhead in a clockwise manner, defend P's hit at the right inner ankle.
- Remaining in the same position, defend P's hit at the left temple with the hit-end.
- Stepping forward with the left foot, defend hit at the right temple with the hit-end.
- Remaining in the same position, defend P's hit at the left inner ankle with the hit-end of the staff.
- Stepping forward with the right foot and changing the grip of the staff as in Fig. 1, defend P's hit on the left temple with the grip-end of the staff.
- Pivot on the left foot by the left and turn full circle and stand facing P, right foot in the rear, and defend P's hit aimed at left outer ankle with the hit-end of the staff. While pivoting, change the grip as in Fig. 2.
- Remaining in the same position, left foot in front, defend P's hit at the right temple with the hit-end of the staff.

Phase 32 - HOLD STAFF WITH LEFT LEADING

Action P and M

- Stand with the left foot leading slightly with a long step. Hold the staff as in Fig. 2, grip-end near the right waist line, hit-end touching the floor in front.

ORAL COMMANDS

Salutation

Hold Staff with Left Leading (Phase 32), Step Right and Hit Ankle (Phase 3), Retreat and Defend Ankle (Phase 4), Cross Hit-Ends (Phase 5)

First Series

A. Step Right and Thrust (1), Retreat and Ward Off Thrust (2), Step Right and Hit Ankle (3), Retreat Right and Defend Ankle (4).

B. Cross Hit ends (5), Hit Left and Right Temples and Left Ankle (6), Defend Thrust, Retreat Left, Defend Temple, Retreat Right, Defend Temple, Defend Ankle and Swirl (7), Cross Hit ends (5), Step Right and Hit Three (8), Step Left and Hit Three (9), Step Right and Hit Three (8), Hit Temple and Ankle (10), Defend Thrust, Retreat Left, Defend Temple, Retreat Right, Defend Temple, Defend Ankle and Swirl (7), Cross Hit ends (5), Step Back Left and Defend Three Hits (11), Step Back Right and Defend Three Hits (12), Step Back Left and Defend Three Hits (11), Hit Temple and Ankle (10), Defend Thrust, Retreat Left, Defend Temple, Retreat Right, Defend Temple, Defend Ankle and Swirl (7), Cross Hit ends (5).

C. Step Right and Hit Three (8), Step Left and Hit Three (9), Step Right and Hit Three (8), Hit Temple and Ankle (10), Defend Thrust, Retreat Left, Defend Temple, Retreat Right, Defend Temple, Defend Ankle and Swirl (7), Cross Hit ends (5), Step Right and Hit Head (13), Step Left and Hit Ankle (14).

Second Series

A. *Repeat B of First Series.*

B. Hit Four and Circle (15).

C. *Repeat C of First Series.*

Third Series

A. *Repeat B of First Series.*

B. Lunge Right and Defend Left Ribs (16), Retreat Right and Defend Right Ribs (17), Retreat Left and Defend Head (18), Retreat Right and Defend Thrust Downward (19), Cross Hit ends (5).

C. *Repeat C of First Series.*

Fourth Series

A. *Repeat B of First Series.*

B. Hit Temple and Turn full circle (20), Hit Temple, Turn full circle and Hit Ankle (21), Cross Hit ends(5).

C. *Repeat C of First Series.*

Fifth Series

A. *Repeat B of First Series.*

B. Lunge Right and Defend Left Ribs (16), Lunge Left and Defend Right Ribs (22), Lunge Right and Defend Left Ribs (16), Retreat Right and Defend Right Ribs (17), Retreat Left and Defend Left Ribs (23), Retreat Right and Defend Right Ribs (17), Retreat Left and Defend Head (18), Retreat Right and Defend Thrust Downward (19), Cross Hit ends (5).

C. *Repeat C of First Series.*

Sixth Series

A. *Repeat B of First Series.*

B. Hit, Jump and Swirl (24), Cross Hit ends (5).

C. *Repeat C of First Series.*

Seventh Series

A. *Repeat B of First Series.*

B. Step Right and Push (25), Step Left and Push (26), Step Right and Push (25), Retreat Right and Push (27), Retreat Left and Push (28), Retreat Right and Push (27), Cross Hit ends (5).

C. *Repeat C of First Series.*

Eighth Series

A. *Repeat B of First Series.*

B. Hit Left and Right Temples and Inner and Outer Ankles (29), Cross Hit ends (5).

C. *Repeat C of First Series.*

Ninth Series

A. *Repeat B of First Series.*

B. Defend Ribs, Head and Chest circling (30), Cross Hit ends (5).

C. *Repeat C of First Series.*

Tenth Series

A. *Repeat B of First Series.*

B. Hit Ankle, Temples, Ankle and Hit pivoting (31), Cross Hit ends (5).

C. *Repeat C of First Series.*

Exercises with the Short Staff (*Muchaan Payattu*)

The *muchaan* or *cheruvati* (short-staff), is normally about three spans long, tapering from the grip-end to the hit-end. Made of tamarind wood or casuarina, the grip-end is about four-and-a-half-inches in circumference while the hit-end is slightly thinner. One could use a cane or bamboo staff to practice the exercises.

The short-staff is a highly manageable and handy weapon, and when wielded with speed it can be effectively employed for defence and attack. Attacks are aimed mostly at the opponent's head, temples, ribs and legs.

Practised in pairs, one taking the role of the master (M), the other that of the pupil (P), the short-staff is wielded at close quarters and so it can be a leathal weapon. Constant practice with the short-staff helps one develop concentration of the mind and lightening reflexes.

While wielding the short-staff, the pupil (P) normally holds it with both hands, the left gripping over the right. The master (M) holds the staff with his right hand, while his left forearm is held slanting across protecting the chest. However, there are occassions when M holds the staff with both hands to add adequate strength to his defence and attack.

Fig.1 Single-handed grip

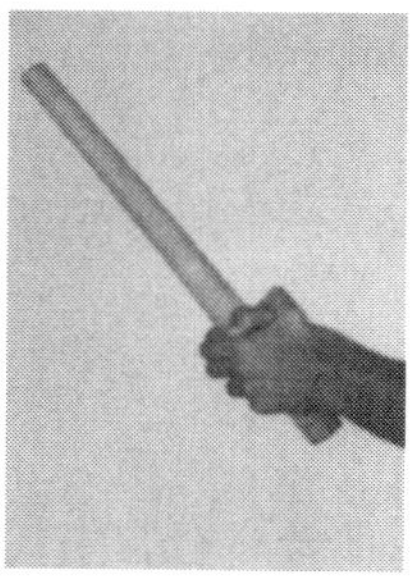

Fig.2 Double-handed grip

PHASES EXPLAINED

- ❑ *Done inside a kalari, M and P stand in the West and East facing each other.*
- ❑ *M and P start the First Series standing in the middle of the kalari.*
- ❑ *M and P start the Series Two to Eight standing in the Eastern end of the kalari.*
- ❑ *The one in white shirt is M; the other in sleeveless vest is P.*

Phase I - STEP RIGHT, HIT SEVEN, STEP BACK

Action P

- Step forward with your right foot and hit M with the hit-end aiming at his left temple twice in quick succession.
- Step back your right foot, swing staff clockwise half circle and hit at M's left lower jaw.
- Then swing the staff anti-clockwise and hit at M's left temple.
- Thereafter, move the hit-end of the staff towards the left and then swing it backwards to hit at M's right temple. Then turn the staff anti-clockwise and hit M's right lower jaw.
- Again hit at M's right temple moving the hit-end of the staff clockwise.

Action M

- Step forward with your right foot and defend P's hits aimed at the left temple in the same manner as P.
- Then step forward with your left foot and defend the rest of the hits in the same order and style as P.

Phase 2 - HIT HEAD BY RIGHT

Action P

- Stepping forward with your right foot, swing the staff overhead from the right side vertically and hit aiming at M's head. Here the staff should travel from behind your back, move over your head and land on M's head.

Action M

- Step backwards with your left foot and bring the staff overhead, slightly to the front, hit-end turned to the right and defend P's hit aimed at the head. The hit is received on the middle portion of the staff

Phase 3 - HIT HEAD BY LEFT

Action P

- Step forward with your left foot and hit aiming at M's head, swinging the staff overhead from the left side vertically. Here the staff should travel from behind your back, move over your head and land on M's head.

Action M

- Step backwards with your right foot and bring the staff overhead, slightly to the front, hit-end turned to the left and defend P's hit aimed at the head. The hit is received on the middle portion of the staff.

Phase 4 - RETREAT LEFT AND DEFEND HEAD

Action P

- Step backwards with your left foot and defend M's hit aimed at the head by raising your staff overhead, slightly to the front, hit-end turned to the right.

Action M

- Step forward with your right foot and hit aiming at P's head.

Phase 5 - DEFEND BELOW INNER RIGHT KNEE

Action P

- Move the hit-end of your staff vertically down through your right side crouching. Plant the hit-end on the floor about six inches left of your right instep and thus defend M's hit aimed below your right knee.

Action M

- Hit aiming below P's right knee.

Phase 6 - RETREAT RIGHT, DEFEND LEFT TEMPLE

Action P

- Step backwards with your right foot and defend M's hit aimed at your left temple.

Action M

- Step forward with your left foot and hit aiming at P's left temple.

Phase 7 - DEFEND RIGHT TEMPLE

Action P

- Defend the hit aimed at your right temple.

Action M

- Hit at P's right temple.

Phase 8 - DEFEND BELOW INNER LEFT KNEE

Action P

- Move the hit end of your staff vertically down through your left side crouching. Plant the hit-end on the floor about six inches right of your left instep and thus defend M's hit aimed below your left knee.

Action M

- Hit below P's inner left knee.

Phase 9 - LIFT AND DEFEND RIGHT TEMPLE

Action P

- Lift your body a little and defend the hit aimed at your right temple.

Action M

- Lift your body a little and hit at P's right temple.

Phase 10 - RETREAT LEFT, DEFEND KNUCKLE

Action P

- Retreat your left foot and elude M's hit aimed at your knuckles. Here hold the staff at your chin-level in front, the hit-end pointing to your right. While defending the attack, pull your fists (holding the staff) towards your left so as to receive M's hit in the middle of the staff.

Action M

- Step forward with your right and hit at P's knuckles at his chin-level.

Phase 11 - RETREAT RIGHT, DEFEND KNUCKLE

Action P

- Retreat your right foot and elude M's hit aimed at your knuckles. Here hold the staff at your chin-level, in front, the hit-end pointing to your left. While defending the attack, pull your fists (holding the staff) towards your right so as to receive M's hit in the middle of the staff.

Action M

- Step forward with the left and hit on P's knuckles at his chin level.

Phase 12 - TROT THRICE

Action P

- Assuming the 'Crouch' posture as in Phase 2 of *Maippayattu* with the left foot in front, trot forward thrice, one following the other.
- While doing this, hold the staff horizontally below your body, the hit-end pointing forward, and supported with the left palm.

Action M

- Facing P and assuming the same posture as P, trot backwards thrice.

Phase 13 - POUNCE ON RIGHT AND HIT HEAD

Action P

- Gripping the staff with both hands, pounce forward and land on the right foot. Hit M in the middle of his head, swinging the staff overhead from the right side.

Action M

- Leap backwards with the left foot behind and defend P's hit holding the staff overhead slightly in front, hit-end turned towards the right.

Phase 14 - RETREAT, JUMP HIGH AND KICK, LEAN, STAFF TUCKED UNDER RIGHT ARMPIT

Action P

- Retreat to reach the starting position. While retreating, guard your chest with your left forearm held inclined in front. The staff is held also in front of your chest, ahead of your left forearm.
- With the right foot in the rear, take off on it and jump high with a scissors kick. While in the air, aim a kick with the outer edge of your right foot at M's right ribs.
- Landing on your left foot, staff tucked under your right armpit, the hit-end pointed backwards, position yourself with a long step, right leg in the rear, body leaning forward.

Action M

- Move forward facing P. While moving forward guard your chest with your left forearm held inclined in front. The staff is held also in front of your chest, ahead of your left forearm.
- With the right foot in front, take off on it and jump high with a scissors kick. While doing this, aim to defend P's kick towards your ribs with the right foot.
- Then land on your left foot, position yourself with a long step, right foot in the rear, body leaning forward.

Phase 15 - STEP RIGHT, DEFEND ABDOMEN

Action P

- Step forward with a long right step thrusting your arms forward. Hold the staff vertically in front of your abdomen (the hit-end of the staff is turned downward, supporting it in the middle with the left palm, fingers turned upward), and thus defend M's hit at your abdomen.

Action M

- Step backwards with your left foot, swing staff horizontally anti-clockwise overhead and hit aiming at P's abdomen, hit-end of the staff turned to the left.

Phase 16 - STEP LEFT, DEFEND ABDOMEN

Action P

- Step forward with a long left, thrust arms forward as in Phase 15, and defend abdomen. While stepping forward, first draw the staff close to your body towards the left armpit and then thrust it forward.

Action M

- Step backwards with your right foot and hit aiming at P's abdomen as in Phase 15.

Phase 17 - RETREAT LEFT, DEFEND BELOW INNER RIGHT KNEE, JUMP AND HIT LEFT AND RIGHT TEMPLE, AND LAND. DEFEND BELOW LEFT INNER KNEE.

Action P

- While retreating left, lift the staff and turn it clockwise and defend M's hit aimed below your inner right knee, hit-end of the staff planted on the floor.
- Then straighten your body, lift your left leg, hold it folded in level with your inner right knee and take off on your right leg, aim a kick at M's right ribs with the outer edge of your right foot with a scissors kick. And then land on your left, right foot a step backwards. While in the air, hit at M's left and right temples.
- Bring down the staff, plant the hit-end on the right side of your left knee to defend M's hit aimed below your left inner knee.

Action M

- Step forward with your right, and hit below P's right inner knee by swinging the staff clockwise.
- Take off on your right leg, aim a kick at P's right ribs with the outer edge of your right foot with a scissors kick. And then land on your left, the right foot a step backwards. While in the air, hit at P's left and right temples.
- Hit below P's left inner knee.

Phase 18 - HIT HEAD FOUR TIMES

Action P

- Step forward with your right, then left, then right and again left hitting M's head as explained in Phase 2 and 3.

Action M

- Step backwards with your left, then right, then left and again right defending P's hits as explained in Phase 2 and 3.

Phase 19 - RETREAT, JUMP HIGH, KICK AND LAND ASTRIDE

Action P

- Retreat to reach the starting position.
- With your right foot in the rear, take off on your right foot and jump high with a scissors kick. While doing this, with the outer edge of your right foot, aim a kick at M's right ribs. Landing on the left, bring your right foot in line with your left foot and stand astride, feet kept a shoulder-width apart.
- Crouch with the staff held vertically in front, the grip-end held in line with your forehead and the hit-end pointed downward held with the left hand clenched-fist facing inward.

Action M

- Move forward facing P. With your right foot in front, do all other movements exactly like P and stand facing him.

Phase 20 - STEP RIGHT, SPRING, SQUAT AND DEFEND LEFT RIBS

Action P

- Step forward with your right foot slightly to the left and spring high with a scissors kick and aim a kick at M's right ribs with your right foot. After the kick, land on your left and assume a 'Squat' posture. (In the 'Squat' posture, your right leg is kept folded behind the body, with the knee touching the ground in front, slightly towards the right, while you sit balancing on your toes and hold the heel of the right foot vertically up).
- While in the' Squat' posture, hold the staff horizontally, the hit-end turned towards your left. The staff is held in line with the chest by holding it on either end with the clenched fists facing downward. Then pull the hit-end towards your body and twist the staff inward and then bringing the hit-end on top and grip-end below. The staff should be held to defend any hits on the left ribs and on the folded left arm.

Action M

- Your action is identical to that of P, except instead of P defending the hit, you hit aiming at P's left ribs.

Front view of P

Phase 21 - DEFEND LEFT INNER KNEE,TWIRL STAFF

Action P

- Remaining in the 'Squat' posture, leave your left hand grip on the hit-end of the staff and grip over the right fist. Then bring down the staff from your left side, anti-clockwise, and defend hit aimed below your left knee. The defence is done by the hit-end of the staff planted on the floor.
- Then scoop M's staff with yours and twirl it towards the left, anti-clockwise, and press it down on the floor.

Action M

- Remaining in the 'Squat' posture, hit below P's left knee, swinging the staff anti-clockwise. Your staff then gets twirled.

Phase 22 - RISE, DEFEND RIGHT TEMPLE

Action P

- Rising from the 'Squat' posture, defend the hit aimed at your right temple by swinging the staff from left to right, your left foot remaining in front.

Action M

- Rising from the 'Squat' posture, aim a hit at P's right temple, your left foot remaining in front.

Phase 23 - ADVANCE HITTING AND DEFENDING

Action P

- With your right foot in front, hit at M's head by swinging the staff overhead.
- Then advance with your left foot and defend M's hit aimed at your head by raising staff overhead, hit-end turned towards the left. Remaining in the same position, again hit at M's head and advance by your right foot. Then defend M's hit aimed at your head by rising staff overhead, hit-end turned towards the right.

Action M

- With your right foot in front, defend P's hit on your head by rising staff overhead, hit-end turned towards the right. Then retreat with your right foot and hit at P's head. Then defend P's hit aimed at your head, remaining in the same position by rising the staff overhead, hit-end turned towards the left.
- Then retreat your left foot and hit at P's head.

Phase 24 - RETREAT HITTING AND DEFENDING

Action P

- With your right foot remaining in front, hit at M's head. Then retreat with your right and defend M's hit aimed at your head with the staff overhead, hit-end turned towards the left. Hit M's head, retreat your left foot, and then defend M's hit aimed at your head with staff overhead, hit-end turned towards the right.

Action M

- With your right foot in front, defend P's hit aimed on to your head holding the staff overhead, hit-end turned towards the right. Advance with your left and hit at P's head, and then defend P's hit on your head by rising staff overhead, hit-end pointing the left. Then advance by your right and hit at P's head.

Phase 25 - STEP RIGHT, DEFEND LEFT RIBS

Action P

- Step forward with your right foot, diagonally slightly to the left and lean forward. While doing this, continue to hold the staff on either end, turn the staff upside down clockwise, and push it forward with the hit-end pointed upwards to defend M's hit aimed at your left ribs.

Action M

- Step backwards with your left foot, leave the grip on the hit-end of the staff, swing it around your shoulders clockwise, and hit at P's left ribs.

Phase 26 - RETREAT RIGHT, DEFEND RIGHT RIBS

Action P

- Step back your right foot. Turn the staff anti-clockwise, push it forward slightly to the right, and defend M's hit aimed at your right ribs, leaning slightly forward. Here the hit-end of the staff should be pointing downward.

Action M

- Step forward with your left foot. Then swing the staff around your shoulders anti-clockwise and hit at P's right ribs.

Phase 27- RETREAT LEFT, DEFEND HEAD PUSHING STAFF UPWARD

Action P

- Step backwards with your left foot. And defend M's hit aimed at your head by pushing the staff horizontally upwards, still holding staff on both ends.

Action M

- Step forward with your right foot. And hit at P's head swinging the staff from the right side.

Phase 28 - RETREAT RIGHT, DEFEND THRUST DOWNWARD

Action P

- Step backwards with your right foot and bring the staff down without changing the grip, in front and defend M's thrust on your abdomen by pushing M's staff downward.

Action M

- Step forward with your left foot and thrust the tip of the hit-end aimed at P's abdomen.

Phase 29 - CIRCLE HITTING AND DEFENDING (HALF CIRCLE, CLOCKWISE)

Action P and M

- In this, both P and M hold the grip-end of the staff with both hands, left gripping over the right as in Fig. 2. Both hit and defend alternatively aiming at each other's head. P hits at M's head and M defends by bringing the staff overhead, slightly to the front, hit-end turned to his right.
- Then M hits aiming at P's head, and P defends it by bringing the staff overhead, slightly to the front, hit-end turned to his left.
- Again P hits aiming at M's head, and M defends the hit as explained earlier, but hit-end turned to.his left.
- Now M hits aiming at P's head and P defends the hit as explained earlier, but hit-end turned to his right.
- P and M perform these movements repeatedly by moving clockwise in half circle, facing each other, and adjusting their paces as is convenient.

Phase 30 - CIRCLE HITTING AND DEFENDING (HALF CIRCLE, ANTI-CLOCKWISE)

Action P and M

- Repeat exactly the same movements as explained in Phase 29, except that while performing them, move anti-clockwise, half a circle.

Phase 31 - STEP LEFT, DEFEND RIGHT RIBS

Action P

- Step forward with your left foot, diagonally slightly to the right and lean forward. While doing this, turn the staff upside down anti-clockwise, and push it forward to defend M's hit aimed at your right ribs. Here the hit-end of the staff should be pointing downward.

Action M

- Step backwards with your right foot, swing the staff around your shoulders anti-clockwise and hit at P's right ribs.

Phase 32 - RETREAT LEFT, DEFEND LEFT RIBS

Action P

- Step back by your left foot. Turn the staff clockwise, push it forward slightly to the left, and defend M's hit aimed at your left ribs, leaning slightly forward. Here the hit-end of the staff should be pointing upward.

Action M

- Step forward with your right foot. Then swing the staff around your shoulders clockwise and hit at P's left ribs.

Phase 33 - CIRCLE HITTING AND DEFENDING (FULL CIRCLE)

Action P and M

- Repeat Phase 29. While doing this, P and M move clockwise, in full circle, facing each other, and adjusting their paces as is convenient.

Phase 34 - ALL PHASES 4 TO 11

Action P and M

- While repeating all Phases 4 to 11, P and M move clockwise in half circle facing each other. While moving, P and M may adjust their paces as is convenient.

Phase 35 - STEP, HIT SEVEN AND CIRCLE

Action P and M

- Repeat Phase I. While doing this, P and M move clockwise in half circle, facing each other. Adjust paces while circling as is convenient.

Phase 36 - STAND WITH LEFT FOOT FORWARD

Action P and M

- With the left foot forward, P and M stand facing each other about ten feet away with a long left step holding the staff with the right hand.

Phase 37 - SLIDE RIGHT SWINGING STAFF

Action P and M

- Folding the right arm and bringing the fist at chest level, swing the staff clockwise vertically on the right side with the wrist rotating. While swinging, step forward with the right foot sliding it in an arcwise manner by the instep of the left foot.

Phase 38 - STEP BACK RIGHT, HOLD STAFF OVERHEAD

Action P and M

- While stepping back with the right foot, lift the staff to hold it near the left temple, hit-end pointing forward. Swing the staff from the left in an anti-clockwise manner aiming a hit at the chin of the opponent in front. Without breaking the flow of the staff, lift it overhead and hold it with both hands, hit-end pointing forward.

Phase 39 - KICK RIGHT AND CROUCH

Action P and M

- Holding the staff overhead, tip pointing forward, aim a kick with the right foot at the opponent in front with the outer edge of the foot, withdraw the foot to the level of the left knee and step forward. While stepping forward, bring down the staff in front of the chest, and assume 'Crouch' posture.

Phase 40 - KICK LEFT AND CROUCH

Action P and M

- Straighten body and hold the staff overhead again. Aim a kick with the left foot at the opponent in front with the outer edge of the foot, and then withdraw the foot to the level of the right knee and step forward. While stepping forward, bring down the staff to be in front of the chest, and assume 'Crouch' posture.

Phase 41 - SQUAT, PROTECT AND BOW

Action P and M

- Squat as in Phase 20. Remaining in the 'Squat' posture, rest the grip-end of the staff on the right thigh with the hit-end resting on the floor. Then cross arms in front of the chest, right over the left, and touch both knees - the left knee with the right and the right knee with the left hand. Then uncross the arms, bring them up to shoulder level, stretched sideways, with palms facing upwards. Thereafter, fold arms and touch shoulders with the fingers. Bring palms together and stretch arms in front at chest level. Then fold arms, palms and forearms close to each other vertically in front of the chest. Then remaining in the 'Squat' posture repeat the movements of the arms twice more.

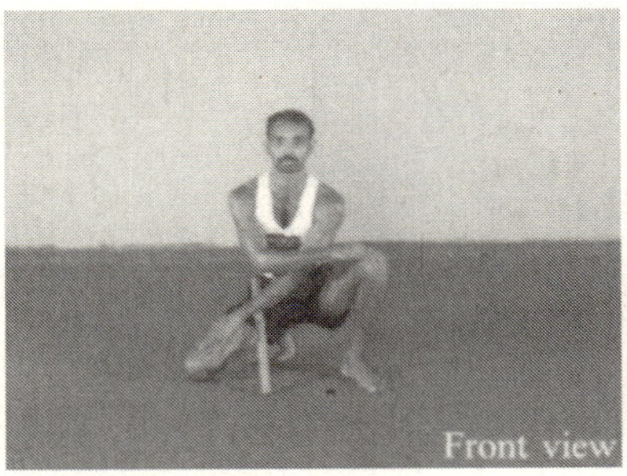

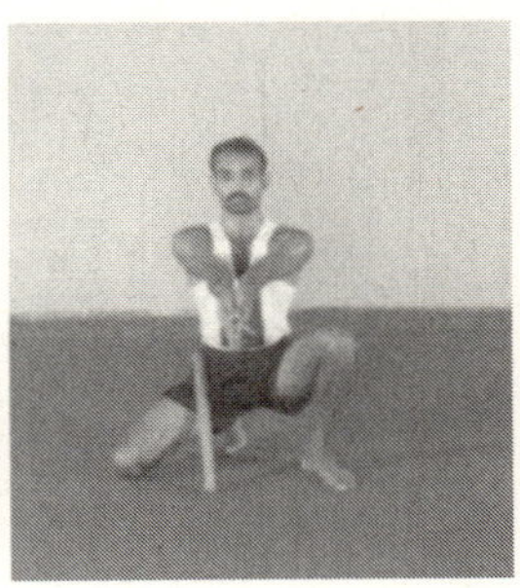

Phase 42 - TOUCH STAFF IN VENERATION

Action P and M

- Touch the staff with the right hand fingers and then touch the head and chest in respectful veneration.

Phase 43 - LIFT STAFF IN VENERATION

Action P and M

- Lift the staff, and hold it upright in front of the chest. Hold the hit-end of the staff with the left hand, palm turned inward. Move the staff in respectful veneration close to the chest.

Phase 44 - BEND FORWARD AND PRESS UP

Action P and M

- Bring the staff down and hold it pressed on the floor with the hit-end pointing forward. Then move body down to the front, chest almost touching the staff, then push up with both hands and straighten body.

Phase 45 - STAND UPRIGHT, MOVE BACK RIGHT FOOT

Action P and M

- From the 'Squat' posture, stand up with the right foot in the rear. While doing this, the staff should be held in the right hand and swung clockwise on the right side with the wrist rotating. Without breaking the flow of the staff execute a hit at the chin of the opponent in front swinging the staff upward from the left side and then hold it on the right side at the waist line with both hands. Meanwhile, move right foot further backwards and crouch turning the body a little to the right.

Phase 46 - STEP RIGHT AND HIT TEMPLE

Action P and M

- Stepping forward with the right foot execute a hit at the left temple. The staff should be lifted to the level of the right shoulder and swung to hit. The staff of both P and M should be meeting mid point.

Phase 47 - RETREAT RIGHT AND CROUCH

Action P and M

- Step right foot backwards by sliding it by the side of the left instep, and crouch. While doing this the staff should be swung overhead and behind the back clockwise and brought to the right waist-line.

Phase 48 - RETREAT RIGHT AND STAND ASTRIDE

Action P and M

- Retreat the right foot and stand astride with the feet a shoulder-width apart and then crouch. While assuming the 'crouch' posture, hold the staff as in Phase 19.

ORAL COMMANDS

Salutation

Stand with Left Foot Forward (Phase 36), Slide Right Swinging Staff (Phase 37), Step Back Right, Hold Staff Overhead (Phase 38), Kick Right and Crouch (Phase 39), Kick Left and Crouch (Phase 40), Squat, Protect and Bow (Phase 41), Touch Staff in Veneration (Phase 42), Lift Staff in Veneration (Phase 43), Bend Forward and Press up (Phase 44), Stand Upright and Move Back Right Foot (Phase 45), Step Right and Hit Temple (Phase 46), Retreat Right and Crouch (Phase 47), Step Right and Hit Temple (Phase 46), Retreat Right and Stand Astride (Phase 48)

First Series

A. Step Right, Hit Seven, Step Back (1), Hit Head by Right (2), Hit Head by Left (3).

B. Retreat Left and Defend Head (4), Defend Below inner Right Knee (5), Retreat Right, Defend Left Temple (6), Defend Right Temple (7), Defend below inner Left Knee (8), Lift and Defend Right Temple (9), Retreat Left, Defend Knuckle (10), Retreat Right, Defend Knuckle (11), Defend Below inner Left Knee (8), Lift and Defend Right Temple (9), Hit Head by Right (2), Hit Head by Left (3).

Normally all the exercises in the First Series (A & B) of the short staff are repeated thrice in continuous succession.

Second Series

A. Trot Thrice (12), Pounce on Right and Hit Head (13), Hit Head by Left (3).

B. Retreat, Jump High and Kick, Lean staff tucked under Right Arm pit (14).

C. Step Right, Defend Abdomen (15), Step Left, Defend Abdomen (16), Step Right, Defend Abdomen (15), Hit Head by Left (3), Hit Head by Right (2), Hit Head by Left (3).

D. *Repeat B of First Series.*

E. *Repeat First Series from start to finish.*

Third Series

A. *Repeat A. of Second Series.*

B. Retreat Left and Defend Head (4), Defend Below inner Right Knee (5), Retreat Right, Defend Left Temple (6), Defend Right Temple (7), Defend below inner Left Knee (8), Lift and Defend Right Temple (9), Retreat Left, Defend Knuckle (10), Retreat Right, Defend Knuckle (11), Defend Below inner Left Knee (8), Lift and Defend Right Temple (9), Retreat Left, Defend Below inner Right Knee, Jump and Hit Left and Right Temple and Land; Defend below Left inner Knee (17), Lift and Defend Right Temple (9).

C. Hit Head four times (18), Step Right, Hit Seven, Step Back (1), Hit Head by Right (2), Hit Head by Left (3).

D. *Repeat B of First Series.*

Fourth Series

A. *Repeat A of Second Series.*

B. Retreat, Jump High, Kick and Land Astride (19), Step Right, Spring, Squat and Defend Ribs (20), Defend Left Inner Knee, Twirl staff (21), Rise, Defend Right Temple (22).

C. *Repeat C of Third Series.*

D. *Repeat B of Third Series.*

E. Hit Head four times (18), Step Right, Hit Seven, Step Back (1), Hit Head by Right (2), Hit Head by Left (3), Retreat Left and Defend Head (4), Advance hitting and defending (23).

F. Retreat hitting and defending (24), Defend Below inner Right Knee (5), Retreat Right, Defend Left Temple (6), Defend Right Temple (7), Defend below inner Left Knee (8), Lift and Defend Right Temple (9), Retreat Left, Defend Knuckle (10), Retreat Right, Defend Knuckle (11), Defend Below inner Left Knee (8), Lift and Defend Right Temple (9).

G. Hit Head by. Right (2), Hit Head by Left (3).

Fifth Series

A. *Repeat A of Second Series.*

B. Retreat, Jump High, Kick and Land Astride (19), Step Right, Defend Left Ribs (25), Retreat Right, Defend Right Ribs (26), Retreat Left, Defend Head pushing staff upward (27), Retreat Right, Defend thrust downward.(28), Step Right, Spring, Squat and Defend Ribs 20), Defend Left inner Knee, Twirl Staff (21), Rise, Defend Right Temple (22).

C. *Repeat C of Third Series.*

D. *Repeat B of Third Series.*

E. Hit Head four times (18), Step Right, Hit Seven, Step Back (1), Hit Head by Right (2), Hit Head by Left (3), Retreat Left and Defend Head (4), Circle hitting and defending (half circle, clockwise) (29), Circle hitting and defending (half circle, anti-clockwise) (30).

F. Defend Below inner Right Knee (5), Retreat Right, Defend Left Temple (6), Defend Right Temple (7), Defend below inner Left Knee (8), Lift and Defend Right Temple (9), Retreat Left, Defend Knuckle (10), Retreat Right, Defend Knuckle (11), Defend Below inner Left Knee (8), Lift and Defend Right Temple (9).

G. *Repeat G of Fourth Series.*

Sixth Series

A. *Repeat A of Second Series.*

B. Retreat, Jump High, Kick and Land Astride (19), Step Right, Defend Left Ribs (25), Step Left, Defend Right Ribs (31), Retreat Left, Defend Left Ribs (32), Retreat Right, Defend Right Ribs (26), Retreat Left, Defend Head pushing staff upwards (27), Retreat Right, Defend Thrust downward (28), Step Right, Spring, Squat and Defend Ribs (20), Defend Left inner Knee, Twirl staff (21), Rise, Defend Right Temple (22).

C. *Repeat C of Third Series.*

D. *Repeat B of Third Series.*

E. Hit Head four times (18), Step Right, Hit Seven, Step Back (1), Hit Head by Right (2), Hit Head by Left (3), Retreat Left and Defend Head (4), Circle hitting and defending (full circle) (33).

E. *Repeat F of Fifth Series.*

F. *Repeat G of Fourth Series.*

Seventh Series

A. *Repeat A of Second Series.*

B. Retreat, Jump High, Kick and Land Astride (19), Step Right, Defend Left Ribs (25), Step Left, Defend Right Ribs (31), Step Right, Defend Left Ribs (25), Retreat Right, Defend Right Ribs (26), Retreat Left, Defend Left Ribs (32), Retreat Right, Defend Right Ribs (26), Retreat Left, Defend Head pushing staff upwards (27), Retreat Right, Defend thrust downward (28), Step Right, Spring, Squat and Defend Ribs (20), Defend Left inner knee, Twirl Staff (21), Rise, Defend Right Temple (22).

C. *Repeat C of Third Series.*

D. *Repeat B of Third Series.*

E. Hit Head four times (18), Step Right, Hit Seven, Step Back (1), Hit Head by Right (2), Hit Head by Left (3), All Phases 4 to 11 (34), Retreat Left, Defend below inner Right Knee, Jump and Hit Left and Right Temple and Land, Defend below left inner Knee (17), Lift and Defend Right Temple (9).

F. *Repeat E above.*

G. Hit Head four times (18), Step Right, Hit Seven, Step Back (1), Hit Head by Right (2), Hit Head by Left (3), Retreat Left and Defend Head (4), Advance hitting and defending (23), Retreat hitting and defending (24), Circle hitting and defending (full circle) (33).

H. *Repeat F of Fifth Series.*

I. *Repeat G of Fourth Series.*

Eighth Series

A. *Repeat A of Second Series.*

B. *Repeat B of Seventh Series.*

C. *Repeat C of Third Series.*

D. *Repeat B of Third Series.*

E. Hit Head four times (18), Step, Hit Seven and Circle (35), Hit Head by Right (2), Hit Head by Left (3).

F. *Repeat B of Third Series.*

G. *Repeat E above.*

H. *Repeat B of Third Series.*

I. Hit Head four times (18), Step Right, Hit Seven, Step Back (1), Hit Head by Right (2), Hit Head by Left (3), Retreat Left and Defend Head (4), Circle hitting and defending (full circle) (33).

J. *Repeat F of Fifth Series.*

K. *Repeat G of Fourth Series.*

EXERCISES WITH THE *OTTA* BATON (*Otta Payatttu*)

Defence and attack using the *otta* are the most advanced in *kolethaari* series. The *otta* is a two-feet long, double curved baton, shaped out of tamarind wood. To prevent the knuckles from being hit during practice, suitable knuckle-guards may be attached to the *otta* baton.

Before setting out to learn how to wield *otta*, the student must have attained a fairly thorough mastery of *maippayattu* and the other series in *kolethaari*. A high degree of physical agility, excellent reflexes, strength and stamina are needed to perform the exercises with perfection.

In this advanced *payattu* technique, the *otta* baton is held differently by M and P. This and the peculiar shape of the baton help add multiplicity to defence and attack styles and inject added force to attacks.

There are regularised techniques of defence and attack in the *otta* series. Yet, depending on the expertise of those wielding this weapon and the circumstances which warrant such action, new techniques of attack and defence to try and trick an opponent to be off-guard may be evolved and employed with deadly effect.

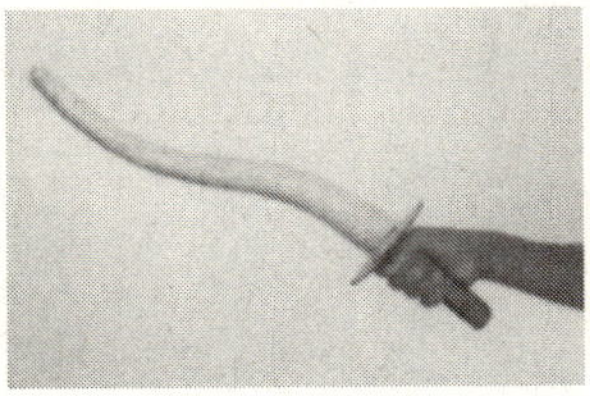

Fig. 1 M's grip

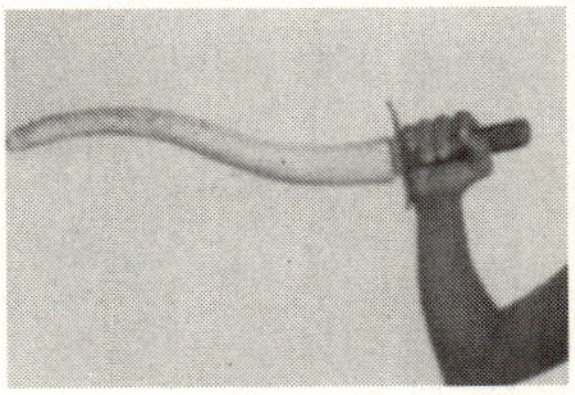

Fig. 2 P's grip

PHASES EXPLAINED

- ❑ *Done inside a kalari* -

a) *M* and P stand in the West and East in the middle of the kalari, about ten feet away facing each other, while starting the Salutation;

b) M and P start Series I and 2 from the eastern end of the kalari;

c) the Series 3 through to 9 all start in the middle of the kalari;

d) the opening exercises in Series 3 through to 9 are called mukham (face) or conceptually the prelude to each.

- ❑ *The one with white wrist bands is M, the other is P.*

Phase I - TROT THRICE AND HIT HEAD POUNCING

Action P

- Stand crouched with the left foot in front.
- Hold the baton in front of the chest supporting it also with the left palm.
- Then trot guardedly forward thrice, left foot leading.
- Then taking off on the left foot, pounce forward, execute a hit with the baton right in the middle of M's head, landing on the right foot in front.

Action M

- Stand crouched with the left foot in front.
- Hold the baton in front of the chest supporting it also with the left palm.
- Then trot guardedly backwards thrice, left foot leading.
- Step back your left foot and defend P's hit by lifting the baton overhead to the front, hit-end turned to the left.

Phase 2 - DEFEND ABDOMEN, SPRING UP, SQUAT AND DEFEND ANKLE

Action P

- Withdraw right foot to the level of the inner left knee, and stepping forward with the right, defend M's hit on the abdomen, hit-end of the baton pointing downward supporting it with the left palm, fingers turned upwards.
- Spring on the right foot and land slightly to the left side on the left foot and squat. While springing up move the baton from the right to left overhead in an anti-clockwise manner and defend M's hit on the left inner ankle in the squatting posture.

Action M

- Withdraw right foot to the level of the inner left knee, and stepping forward with the right, hit at P's abdomen hit-end pointing towards the left.
- Spring on the right foot and land slightly to the left side on the left foot and squat. While springing up move the baton from the right to left overhead in an anti-clockwise manner and hit P's left inner ankle in the squatting posture.

Phase 3 - RISE UP AND HIT RIGHT TEMPLE

Action P and M

- Rise up with the left foot in front, and hit at the right temple swinging the hit-end of the baton from the left to the right.

Phase 4 - RETREAT, JUMP HIGH AND KICK, LEAN WITH A LONG STEP

Action P

- Retreat to reach the starting position.
- With the right foot in the rear, take off on it and jump high with a scissors kick. Landing on the left, keep right foot back with a long step and lean forward.

Action M

- Move forward facing P.
- With the right foot in front, take off on it and jump high with a scissors kick. Landing on the left foot, keep right foot back with a long step and lean forward.

Phase 5 - STEP RIGHT AND DEFEND HEAD

Action P

- Stepping forward with the right, defend M's hit at the head by lifting the baton overhead slightly to the front hit-end pointing towards the left.
- Support the baton with the left palm, fingers pointing to the right.

Action M

- Stepping forward with the right, hit at P's head with the baton, swinging it from the right.

Phase 6 - THRUST (RIGHT LEADING)

Action P

- Remaining in the same position with the right foot leading, withdraw the baton to the right side, and then thrust at M's chest.

Action M

- Remaining in the same position with the right foot leading, ward off P's thrust by snapping down your baton with the hit-end pointing to the right.

Phase 7 - HIT RIGHT TEMPLE

Action P

- Remaining in the same position with the right foot leading, hit at M's right temple with the hit-end swinging the baton upwards.

Action M

- Remaining in the same position with the right foot leading, hit at P's right temple, swinging the baton upwards.

Phase 8 - STEP LEFT, SQUAT AND HIT ANKLE

Action P

- Step forward with the left foot and squat.
- While stepping forward, swing the baton from the right to left in front, anti-clockwise, and hit M's inner left ankle in the squatting posture.

Action M

- Step backwards with the right foot and squat.
- While stepping backwards, swing the baton from the right to left in an anti-clockwise manner in front, and defend P's hit aimed at the inner left ankle.

Phase 9 - TROT BACK AND CROUCH

Action P

- Rise up, trot back and crouch with the left foot leading, baton held in front of the chest.

Action M

- Rise up, trot forward with the left foot leading. Face P in the 'Crouch' posture.

Phase 10 - THRUST (LEFT LEADING)

Action P

- Stand up and with the left foot leading, aim a thrust at M's chest with the tip of the baton.

Action M

- Stand up and with the left foot leading, ward off P's thrust as in Phase 6.

Phase 11 - STEP RIGHT AND THRUST

Action P

- Step forward with the right foot and aim a thrust at M's chest with the tip of the baton.

Action M

- Step backwards with the left foot and ward off P's thrust as in Phase 6.

Phase 12 - DEFEND ABDOMEN, SPRING UP, SQUAT, DEFEND ANKLE AND SWIRL

Action P

- Repeat Phase 2 and after the hit on the ankle, scoop and swirl M's baton towards the left and press it down.

Action M

- Repeat Phase 2 and after the hit on the ankle, your baton gets scooped and swirled.

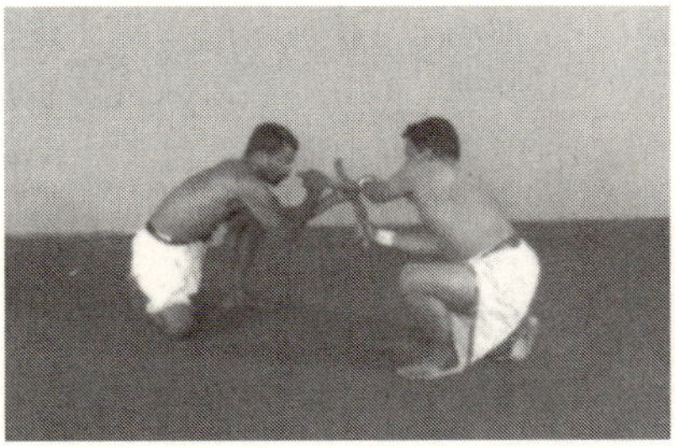

Phase 13 - STAND UP, STEP BACK TWICE

Action P

- Stand up and step back with the left foot and then with a long right step. While doing this, hold baton guarding your chest.

Action M

- Stand up and step forward with the right and then with a long left step. While doing this, hold the baton guarding your chest.

Phase 14 - STEP LEFT AND HIT TEMPLE

Action P

- Step forward with the left foot.
- Turn the body slightly towards the right, swing a hit at M's left temple. While swinging the baton, add force to the hit by turning the body and hip to face M.

Action M

- Stepping back with the right foot, defend P's hit at the left temple with the same movement as P.

Phase 15 - STEP RIGHT AND HIT THREE

Action P

- Step forward with the right, turn body slightly to the left, and aim a hit at M's right temple, then the lower chin and again at the right temple in succession.

Action M

- Step back with the left foot, turn body slightly to the left and defend the three hits by moving baton the same way as P.

Phase 16 - STEP LEFT AND DEFEND ABDOMEN

Action P

- Step forward with the left foot and defend M's hit at the abdomen.
- While defending, the baton should be held vertically in front of the abdomen, hit-end pointing downward supported with the left palm, fingers pointing upwards.

Action M

- Stepping backwards with the right, hit at P's abdomen with the baton, the hit-end turned horizontally to the left.

Phase 17 - STEP LEFT AND HIT ANKLE

Action P

- Step left foot forward, swing baton in front of the body anti-clockwise, crouch and hit at M's left inner ankle.

Action M

- Stepping backwards with the right foot and swinging the baton in front of the body anti-clockwise, crouch and defend P's hit at the left inner ankle.

Phase 18 - HIT HEAD BY RIGHT

Action P

- Step forward with the right foot and hit at M's head swinging baton from your right side.

Action M

- Step backwards with the left foot and defend P's hit on the head rising baton overhead slightly to the front, hit-end pointing towards the left, the baton supported with the left palm.

Phase 19 - RETREAT RIGHT AND DEFEND HEAD

Action P

- Retreat right foot, lift the baton overhead with the hit-end turned to the left to defend M's hit aimed on the head. Support the baton with your left palm, fingers pointed towards the right.

Action M

- Stepping forward with the left foot, aim a hit on P's head, swinging the baton from the right side.

Phase 20 - STEP RIGHT AND HIT ANKLE

Action P

- Stepping forward with the right, crouch, and swing the baton from the right shoulder-level and aim a hit at M's right inner ankle.

Action M

- Stepping backwards with the left foot, crouch, and defend the hit from P at the right inner ankle by swinging the baton from the right shoulder-level downward.

Phase 21 - RETREAT RIGHT AND DEFEND ANKLE

Action P

- Retreat right foot and defend M's hit at the inner left ankle in the crouch posture. While retreating, the baton should be swung anti-clockwise in front of the body.

Action M

- Step forward with the left foot, and hit at P's left inner ankle by swinging the baton anti-clockwise in front of the body, assuming the 'crouch' posture.

Phase 22 - DEFEND ABDOMEN

Action P

- Remaining with the left foot in front, stand up and defend M's hit at the abdomen holding the baton with both hands, tip pointing downward.

Action M

- Remaining with the left foot in front, stand up and aim a hit at P's abdomen, tip of the baton pointing towards the left.

Phase 23 - DEFEND ABDOMEN AND CHEST

Action P

- Stand with the left foot leading.
- Hold the baton with both hands in front of the chest, hit-end pointing downward, slightly towards the left. Remaining in the same posture, defend the two repeated hits of M at the abdomen by stretching the hands forward.
- Then step forward with the right foot and ward off M's thrust at the chest downwards by swinging the baton in an anti-clockwise manner in front of your chest.

Action M

- With the left foot in front, hit twice repeatedly at P's abdomen with the hit-end of the baton turned to the left.
- Then stepping backwards with the left foot, thrust at P's chest with the point of the baton.

Phase 24 - DEFEND HIT WITH RIGHT IN FRONT

Action P

- Remaining with the right foot in front, lift baton overhead slightly to the front, tip pointing towards the left and defend M's hit aimed at the head. Support the baton with your left palm, fingers pointed towards the right.

Action M

- Remaining with the right foot in front, aim a hit at P's head with the baton.

Phase 25 - PLANT BATON AND DEFEND ANKLE

Action P

- Remaining with the right foot leading, crouch and defend M's hit on the right inner ankle, planting the tip of the baton on the floor in front.

Action M

- Remaining with the right foot in front, crouch and hit P's right inner *ankle*.

Phase 26 - HIT TEMPLE WITH RIGHT FOOT IN FRONT

Action P

- With the right foot remaining in front, aim a hit at M's left temple with the hit-end of the baton with an upward swing.

Action M

- Remaining with the right foot in front, defend P's hit aimed at the left temple by swinging the baton towards the left.

Phase 27 - STEP LEFT, DEFEND ABDOMEN AND HIT RIGHT TEMPLE

Action P

- Stepping forward with the left foot, hold baton, tip pointing downward and defend hit on the abdomen. In succession, remaining in the same position, execute a hit at M's right temple.

Action M

- Stepping backwards with the right foot, hit at P's abdomen and defend hit at the right temple.

Phase 28 - STEP RIGHT DEFEND ABDOMEN AND HIT RIGHT TEMPLE

Action P

- Stepping forward with the right foot, hold baton, tip pointing downward, and defend hit on the abdomen. In succession, remaining in the same position, execute a hit at M's right temple.

Action M

- Stepping backwards with the left foot, hit at P's abdomen and defend hit at the right temple.

Phase 29 - HIT TEMPLE, CLOSE IN AND RISE

Action P and M

- Remaining in the 'squat' posture, aim a hit at the right temple.
- Hold the baton in that position supporting it with the left hand, and rise up.
- With a long left step forward, close-in chest to chest, lifting the baton overhead stretching the arms.

Phase 30 - KICK RIB AND SIT

Action P and M

- Rising from the closing position of Phase 29, aim a kick at the right ribs with the right leg, and then sit back on the right foot with a long backwards step as in Phase 41 of *Maippayattu*.

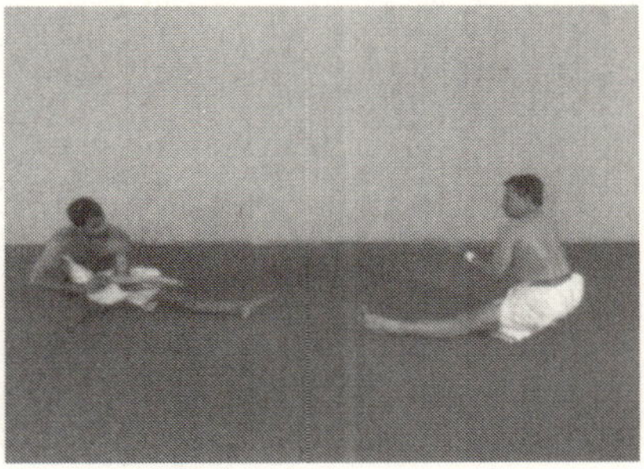

Phase 31 - STAND UP, STEP RIGHT AND THRUST

Action P and M

- Rising from Phase 30, repeat Phase 11.

Phase 32 - LEAN WITH A LONG STEP

Action P and M

- With the left foot in front with a long step P and M stand ten feet apart facing each other.

Phase 33 - SWING RIGHT OUTWARD, STAND ASTRIDE AND SPRING

Action P and M

- Swing right leg outward (as in Phase 23 of M*aippayattu*) and stand astride. Then spring up and execute a high kick in front with the right foot and land on the left foot. Keep right foot in the rear and crouch.

Phase 34 - RETREAT LEFT AND RIGHT, DEFEND THRUST, SQUAT AND DEFEND ANKLE

Action P

- In the 'Crouch' posture, retreat left foot and right foot defending two thrusts of M aimed at the chest by pushing them downwards. Then squat and defend M's hit on the left inner ankle.

Action M

- In the 'Crouch' posture, step forward with the right foot and then left, aiming two thrusts at P's chest. Then squat and hit at P's left inner ankle.

Phase 35 - STEP LEFT AND HIT RIGHT TEMPLE

Action P

- Step forward with a long left step and hit at M's right temple and hold baton in that position supported by the left palm.

Action M

- Step backwards with a long right step and defend P's hit at the right temple and hold baton in that position supported by the left palm.

Phase 36 - RETREAT LEFT AND DEFEND HEAD

Action P

- Retreat with the left foot and defend M's hit on the head by lifting the baton overhead slightly to the front, hit-end pointing to the left.

Action M

- Step forward with the right foot and hit at P's head.

Phase 37 - RETREAT RIGHT, SQUAT, DEFEND ANKLE AND SWIRL

Action P

- Retreat with the right foot and squat. While retreating swing the baton anti-clockwise in front of the body and defend M's hit aimed at the left inner ankle in the 'squat' posture. Then supporting the baton with your left hand, scoop M's baton, and press it down on the left with a swirl.

Action M

- Step forward with the left foot and squat. While stepping forward, swing the baton anti-clockwise overhead, and execute a hit at P's left inner ankle while squatting. Then your baton gets scooped up and swirled.

Phase 38 - THRUST

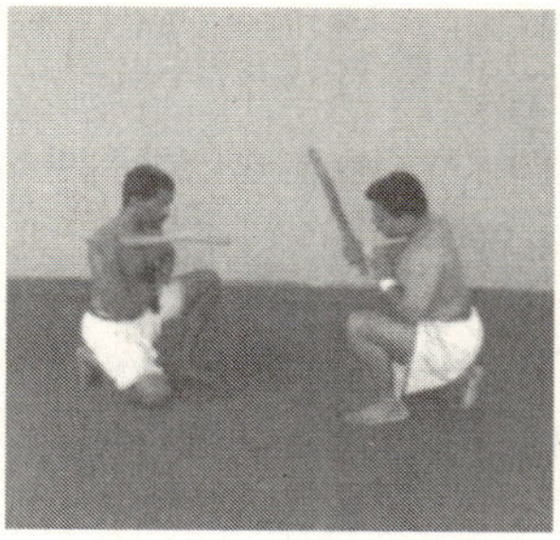

Action P

- Remaining in the 'squat' posture, aim a thrust at M's chest with the tip of the baton.

Action M

- Remaining in the 'squat' posture, ward off P's thrust downwards to the right side.

Phase 39 - HIT RIGHT TEMPLE SQUATTING

Action P

- Remaining in the same 'squat' posture, aim a hit at M's right temple.

Action M

- Remaining in the same 'squat' posture, defend P's hit aimed at the right temple.

Phase 40 - STAND UP AND HIT TEMPLE

Action P

- Rising up from the 'squat' posture, with the left foot still in front, turn body slightly to the right, and swing a hit at M's left temple with the movement of the hip to add strength to the hit.

Action M

- Rising up from the 'squat' posture, with the left foot still in front, defend P's hit at the left temple with the same movement as P.

Phase 41 - CROUCH WITH LEFT FOOT IN FRONT

Action P and M

- With the left foot leading, crouch facing each other with the baton held guarding the chest.

Phase 42 - RETREAT CROUCHING

Action P and M

- Facing each other with the left foot leading, in the 'crouch' posture, slowly retreat six steps.

Phase 43 - KICK RIGHT AND CROUCH

Action P and M

- Stand up. Hold the baton overhead with both hands, tip pointing forward.
- Kick high in front with the outer edge of the right foot.
- Withdraw the foot to the level of the left knee and step forward. While stepping forward, the baton should be brought down to be in front of the chest and then assume the 'crouch' posture.
  (This is normally done in slow motion to give it an agile grace.)

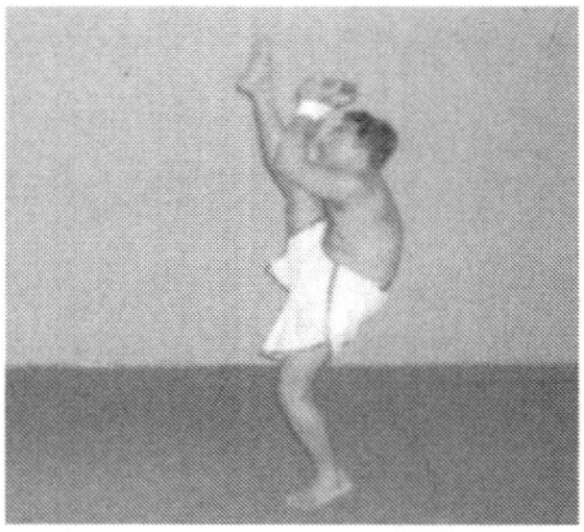

Phase 44 - KICK LEFT AND CROUCH

Action P and M

- Stand up. Hold the baton overhead with both hands, tip pointing forward.
- Kick high in front with the outer edge of the left foot.
- Withdraw the foot to the level of the right knee and step forward. While stepping forward, the baton should be brought down to be in front of the chest and assume the 'crouch' posture.
  (This is normally done in slow motion to give it an agile grace.)

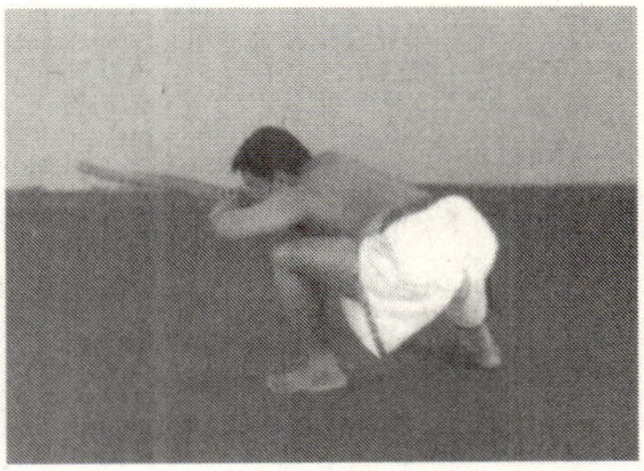

Phase 45 - KICK LEFT HIGH, STEP AND LEAP

Action P and M

- Repeat Phase 6 and 7, 13 and 14 and 7 of *maippayattu* with the baton held in front. While doing these, P and M will cross each other through their right-hand side, and proceed further. At the end of these, P and M will stand apart with their backs turned to each other, and not facing each other.

Phase 46 - RETREAT AND HIT LEG

Action P and M

- Retreating and while the right shoulders of both come in line, P and M hit at each other's right calf with the batons moving backwards.

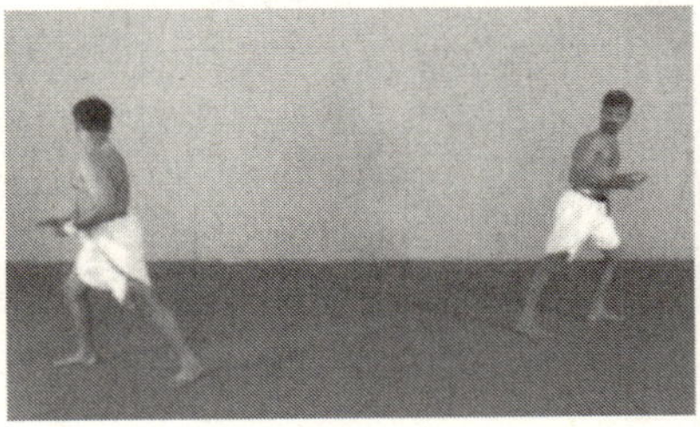

Phase 47 - RETREAT RIGHT, STAND ASTRIDE AND JUMP

Action P and M

- Step back with the right foot and stand astride facing each other. Taking off on both feet, jump up and aim a kick with the right foot at each other's right ribs, land on the left foot and stand with a long step, right foot in the rear.

Phase 48 - STEP RIGHT, DEFEND TEMPLE, JUMP AND TURN

Action P

- Step forward with the right foot diagonally slightly towards the left. Ward off M's hit aimed at the left temple by swinging the baton from the left to right in front of the face with the tip pointing upwards.
- In succession take off on the right foot, jump forward and land on the left foot, turn to the right and stand facing M with a long right step backwards.

Action M

- Hitting at P's left temple, repeat all the movements as P.

Phase 49 - STEP RIGHT AND LEFT, TURN AND HIT ANKLES

Action P and M

- Step forward with the right foot and then left, and press the batons crossed against each other, hit-end pointing slightly upwards.
- Lift the batons overhead by pressing them against each other and step forward with the right foot. Simultaneously, return to the original position as at the start of Phase 48, and face each other with the left foot in front.
- Hit outer and inner ankle of the left foot in quick succession.

Phase 50 - RETREAT RIGHT AND CROUCH

Action P and M

- Step back with the right foot and assume the 'crouch' posture. While retreating withdraw the baton overhead anti-clockwise and hold it in front of the chest.

Phase 51 - STEP RIGHT, DEFEND TEMPLE, TURN AND HIT ANKLES

Action P

- Step forward with the right foot diagonally slightly towards the left and defend M's hit at the left temple by lifting the baton from the right side upwards.
- Step forward with the left foot and cross M by the right side. Turn to the opposite direction by the right and face M, keeping the right foot in the rear with a long step.
- Hit left inner ankle and outer ankle in quick succession.

Action M

- Hitting P's left temple, repeat all the movements as P.

Phase 52 - RETREAT AND HIT TEMPLE

Action P and M

- Retreating and while crossing each other and when the right shoulders of both come in line, P and M hit at each other's right temple with the batons moving backwards.

Phase 53 - STRAIGHT RIGHT AND SIT

Action P and M

- Repeat Phase 41 of *maippayattu* with the baton held in front of the chest.

Phase 54 - STRAIGHT LEFT AND SIT

Action P and M

- Repeat Phase 42 of *maippayattu* with the baton held in front of the chest.

Phase 55 - OUTWARD RIGHT

Action P and M

- Standing astride and without stepping left foot forward, repeat Phase 23 of *maippayattu* with the baton held closely in front of the chest.

Phase 56 - OUTWARD LEFT

Action P and M

- Standing astride and without stepping right foot forward, repeat Phase 24 of *maippayattu* with the baton held closely in front of the chest.

Phase 57 - SQUAT AND HIT ANKLE

Action P

- Squat on the right foot in the rear and hit M's left inner ankle.

Action M

- Squat on the right foot in the rear and defend P's hit on the left inner ankle.

Phase 58 - RETREAT, JUMP AND TURN

Action P and M

- Turn by the right to the opposite direction, jump forward taking off on the right foot and land on the left. While landing on the left, turn by the right to the opposite direction and stand facing each other leaning forward with a long right step backwards.

Phase 59 - SLIDE RIGHT, SCISSORS KICK AND LEAN

Action P and M

- Repeat 'Slide Right and Scissors Kick' movement of Phase 56 of *maippayattu*. While in mid-air doing scissors kick, hit at each other's right temple with the baton. Then stand facing each other leaning forward with a long right step backwards.

Phase 60 - STEP RIGHT, RECEIVE HIT AND WARD OFF

Action P

- Stepping forward with the right foot, defend M's hit on the head as in Phase 5, and then ward off M's baton towards the right side with an arc-wise motion.

Action M

- Stepping forward with the right foot, hit at P's head.

Phase 61 - STEP FORWARD AND THRUST

Action P

- Stepping forward with the left and without breaking the flow of the baton, execute a thrust with the tip of the baton at M's chest.

Action M

- Stepping backwards with the right foot, swing the baton downward and ward off P's thrust towards the right side.

Phase 62 - RETREAT LEFT AND DEFEND CHEST

Action P

- Step backwards with the left foot and press down M's thrust by snapping the baton downwards.

Action M

- Stepping forward with the right foot aim a thrust at P's chest with the tip of the baton.

Phase 63 - STEP RIGHT, DEFEND TEMPLE, JUMP, TURN AND HIT ANKLES

Action P

- Step forward with the right foot diagonally slightly to the left. Defend M's hit on the left temple by lifting the baton from the right to left.
- Take off on the right foot and turning slightly by the right side aim a scissors kick with the right foot at M's right ribs. While in mid air during the scissors kick, hit at M's right temple.
- Land on the left foot forward, turn by the right to stand facing M with a long right step backwards. Hit left inner ankle and outer ankle in quick succession leaning body forward.

Action M

- Repeat the same movements as P executing the first hit and defending the second.

Phase 64 - TURN AND HIT ANKLES

Action P and M

- Withdraw the left foot towards the right knee and lounge forward with the left foot and press batons crossed against each other. Then repeat, Turn and Hit Ankles' as in Phase 49.

Phase 65 - SQUAT, DEFEND ANKLE AND SWIRL

Action P

- Squat on the right foot in the rear, defend M's hit on the left inner ankle and scoop and swirl M's baton towards the left and press it down.

Action M

- Squat on the right foot in the rear, hit at P's left inner ankle. Your baton gets scooped and swirled.

Phase 66 - HIT THRICE SQUATTING

Action P and M

- Repeat Phase 15 remaining in the 'squat' posture.

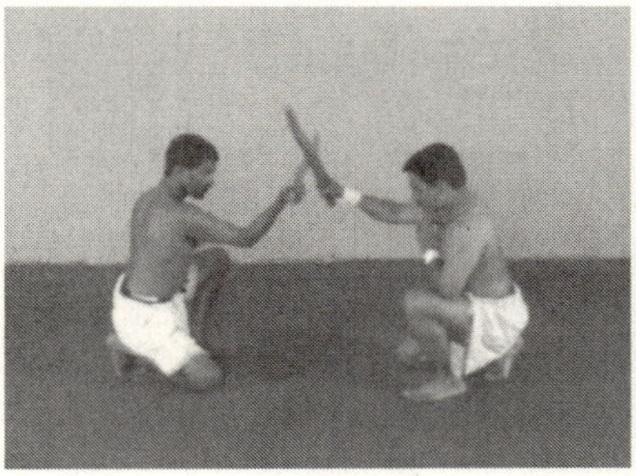

Phase 67 - DEFEND CHEST RETREATING TWICE

Action P

- In the 'crouch' posture, step back left and then right foot and defend M's two thrusts aimed at the chest by pushing M's baton down with your baton, hit-end turned towards the left.

Action M

- In the 'crouch' posture, step forward with the right and then left foot, and aim two thrusts at P's chest with the tip of the baton.

Phase 68 - DEFEND HEAD, JUMP AND DEFEND CHEST

Action P

- Remaining with the left foot in front, stamp right foot in the rear and take off on it and execute a scissors kick in front with the right foot aiming at M's right ribs. Land on the left foot and keep the right behind and crouch. While doing the scissors kick, defend M's hit at the head while in mid air. While landing press M's thrust at your chest downward.

Action M

- Here your action is identical to that of P, except that you hit and thrust at P.

Phase 69 - RETREAT LEFT AND SWING UP BATON

Action P

- Retreat by the left foot and ward off M's thrust aimed at the chest by swinging the baton upward clockwise.

Action M

- Step forward with the right foot and aim a thrust at P's chest with the tip of the baton.

Phase 70 - RETREAT, JUMP AND SIT BACK

Action P and M

- Retreat and after hitting at the right temple and crossing each other, step right foot astride, take off on both feet and jump high with a scissors kick. Landing on the left foot sit back as in Phase 41 of *maippayattu.*

Phase 71 - OUTWARD RIGHT, SIT SIDEWAYS AND REPEAT

Action P and M

- Stand astride and swing right foot outward as in Phase 23 of *maippayattu.* Then slide the right foot further to the right with a long step. Sit on it holding the left foot stretched towards the left.
- Rising up slightly, swing the body backwards half circle from left to right as in Phase 45 of *maippayattu* and shift the sitting position on to the left foot. While doing this, the baton should be held overhead with both hands. The right leg should be stretched on your right side.

- Rising up slightly, swing the body backwards as in Phase 45 of *maippayattu* and sit on the right foot. While doing this, hold the baton overhead with both hands. The left foot should remain stretched on the left side.

Phase 72 - WITHDRAW TURNING

Action P and M

- Turn by the right to the opposite direction and step forward with the left foot. Again turn by the right to the opposite direction and moving right foot through the rear step right backwards with a long step and face each other.

Phase 73 - STEP RIGHT AND LEFT AND CROSS BATONS

Action P and M

- Step forward with the right foot and then left, and press the batons crossed against each other, hit-end pointing slightly upwards to the left.

Phase 74 - STEP LEFT AND THRUST DEEP

Action P

- Stepping forward with the left foot, turn body slightly towards the right. Then sally a thrust at M's chest. Add force to the hit with an appropriate swing of your body and hip.

Action M

- Stepping back with the right foot, ward off P's thrust by swinging the baton downwards.

Phase 75 - RETREAT AND ROTATE BATON

Action P

- Step back with the right foot and defend hit at the left temple and rotate M's baton downward and then towards the right in a single quick flowing motion.

Action M

- Stepping forward with the left foot, aim a hit at P's left temple.

Phase 76 - DEFEND ANKLE AND SWIRL

Action P

- Remaining crouched and with the right foot in the rear, defend M's hit at the inner left ankle as in Phase 21 and then scoop up M's baton and swirl it towards the left side.

Action M

- Remaining crouched and with the left foot in front, hit at P's left inner ankle. Your baton gets scooped up and swirled.

Phase 77 - TURN, HIT ANKLES AND SWIRL

Action P

- Repeat Phase 64 and after hitting at the ankles, scoop up M's baton and swirl it towards the left side.

Action M

- Repeat Phase 64. Your baton gets scooped and swirled.

Phase 78 - STAND UP, JUMP AND HIT TEMPLES

Action P and M

- From the 'squat' posture, stand up and taking off on the right foot, execute a scissors kick in front. While in mid air hit at each other's left and right temples in quick succession.

Phase 79 - RETREAT RIGHT AND CLOSE IN CHEST

Action P and M

- P retreats the right foot with a long step and M steps forward with a long left. Simultaneously, they press the batons held with both hands crossed in front of the chest. Then while lifting the batons overhead, they close in with the chest against each other.

Phase 80 - RETREAT LEFT AND DEFEND ANKLE

Action P

- Step back with the left foot and defend M's hit at the right inner ankle.

Action M

- Step forward with the right foot and hit at P's right inner ankle.

Phase 81 - DEFEND HEAD AND WARD OFF

Action P

- Remaining in the 'squat' posture, defend M's hit on the head and then ward off M's baton towards the right side with an arc wise motion.

Action M

- Remaining in the 'squat' posture, hit at P's head.

Phase 82 - PRESS DOWN BATON

Action P

- After defending M's thrust downward in the 'squat' posture, in a rapid action lift baton, turn the hit-end towards the right and press M's baton on to the floor. The right-grip is turned downward and the left palm supports the baton crossed over the right arm.

Action M

- Remaining in the 'squat' posture thrust at P's chest

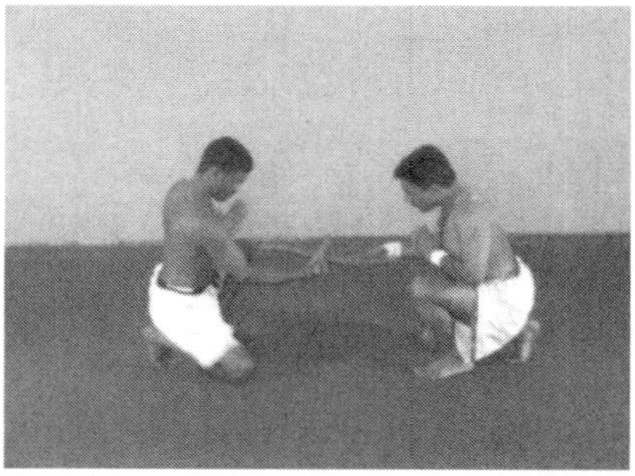

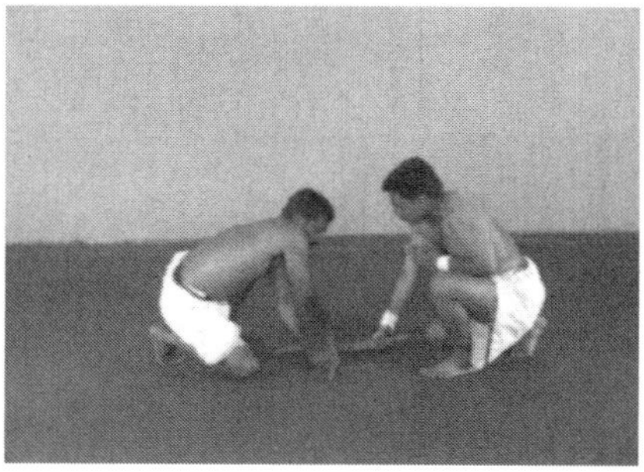

Phase 83 - STAND WITH LEFT FOOT FORWARD

Action P and M

- With a long left foot forward, P and M stand facing each other about ten feet away, holding the baton with the right hand, guarding the chest.

Phase 84 - STEP RIGHT AND TOUCH FLOOR IN VENERATION

Action P and M

- Step right foot forward and swing the baton once clockwise in front of the chest with your right arm stretched, and touch the floor in front with the tip of the baton in veneration. Your left arm remains guarding the chest.

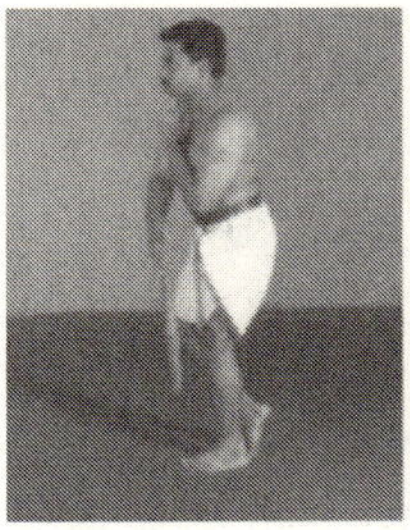

Phase 85 - SQUAT

Action P and M

- Squat on the right foot.

Phase 86 - BEND FORWARD AND PRESS UP

Action P and M

- Hold the baton in front of the body vertically, hit-end pointing upwards. Bring the baton down and hold it pressed on the floor with the tip pointing forward.
- Then lower the body down to the front, chest almost touching the baton, then push up with both hands and straighten body.

Phase 87 - PROTECT AND BOW

Action P and M

- Remaining in the 'squat' position, rest the grip-end of the baton on the right thigh with the hit-end resting on the floor.
- Cross arms in front of the chest, right over the left, and touch both the knees, the right knee with the left and the left knee with the right.
- Uncross the arms, bring them to shoulder level, stretched sideways, with the palms facing upwards.
- Then fold arms and touch shoulders with the fingers.
- Bring the arms pressed together in front of your chest, stretch arms forward at chest level.
- Fold arms and hold them in front of the chest with the forearms vertically together. Bend your body backwards, the folded arms still held close to the chest. Bring body forward and straighten it, the folded arms still in position. (Repeat these movements of the hands three times.)
- Touch the baton with your right hand, then your forehead and chest in respectful veneration. Then lift the baton with your right hand, hold it upright in front of your chest as in Phase 85. Hold the hit-end of the baton with your left hand, palm turned inward. Pull the baton close to your chest.

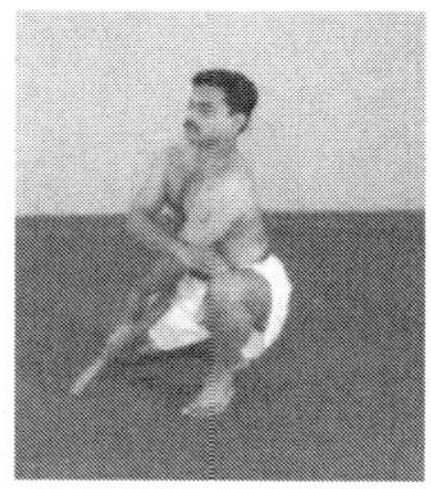

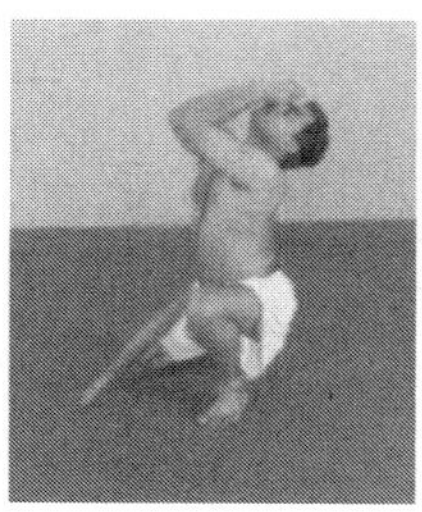

Phase 88 - RETREAT LEFT AND RIGHT CROUCHING

Action P and M

- Assume 'crouch' posture and retreat left and right.

Phase 89 - SLIDE RIGHT FOOT, SWING LEFT FOOT INWARD, TROT BACK AND CROUCH

Action P

- Step right foot forward by sliding it in an arc-wise manner by the side of the left instep. Swing left foot high inward in front and keep it on the right side slightly behind turning the body to the right.
- Then take off on the left foot, trot back and crouch with the right foot in the rear.

Action M

- Step right foot forward by sliding it in an arc-wise manner by the side of the left instep. Kick high with the outer edge of the left foot and withdraw it to the level of the right knee. Then step left foot forward and take off on that and trot forward to land on the right with the left foot leading. Assume the 'crouch' posture with the left foot leading.

Phase 90 - STAND UP

Action P and M

- Stand up with the left foot still in front.

ORAL COMMANDS

Salutation

Stand with Left Foot Forward (Phase 83), Step Right and Touch Floor in Veneration (Phase 84), Kick Right and Crouch (Phase 43), Kick Left and Crouch (Phase 44), Squat (Phase 85), Bend Forward and Press Up (Phase 86), Protect and Bow (Phase 87), Bend Forward and Press Up (Phase 86), Retreat Left and Right Crouching (Phase 88), Slide Right Foot, Swing Left Foot Inward, Trot Back and Crouch (Phase 89)

First Series

A. Trot thrice and Hit Head pouncing (Phase 1), Defend Abdomen, Spring up, Squat and Defend Ankle (2), Rise Up and Hit Right Temple (3).

B. Retreat, Jump High and Kick, Lean with a Long Step (4).

C. Step Right and Defend Head (5), Thrust (right leading) (6), Hit Right Temple (7), Step Left, Squat and Hit Ankle (8), Rise Up and Hit Right Temple (3), Trot Back and Crouch (9).

D. Thrust (left leading) (10), Step Right and Thrust (11), Hit Right Temple (7), Defend Abdomen, Spring Up, Squat, Defend Ankle and Swirl (12), Stand Up, Step back twice (13).

E. Step Right and Defend Head (5), Thrust (right leading) (6), Hit Right Temple (7), Step Left and Hit Temple (14), Step Right and Hit Three (15), Step Left and Defend Abdomen (16), Step Right and Thrust (11), Step Left and Hit Ankle (17), Hit Head by Right (18), Defend Abdomen, Spring Up, Squat and Defend Ankle (2), Rise Up and Hit Right Temple (3).

F. Retreat, Jump High and Kick, Lean with a Long Step (4).

G. Step Right and Defend Head (5), Retreat Right and Defend Head (19), Step Right and Hit Ankle (20), Retreat Right and Defend Ankle (21), Defend Abdomen (22), Defend Abdomen and Chest (23) (three times), Defend Hit with Right in Front (24), Thrust (right leading) (6), Hit Right Temple (7), Plant baton and Defend Ankle (25), Hit Temple with Right Foot in front (26), Hit Right Temple (7), Step Left, Defend Abdomen and Hit Right Temple (27), Step Right, Defend Abdomen and Hit Right Temple (28), Step Left and Hit Ankle (17), Retreat Left and Defend Head (36), Retreat Right and Defend Ankle (21), Hit Head by Right (18), Defend Abdomen, Spring Up, Squat and Defend Ankle (2), Rise Up and Hit Right Temple (3).

H. Retreat, Jump High and Kick, Lean with a Long Step (4).

I. Step Right and Defend Head (5), Retreat Right and Defend Head (19), Step Right and Hit Ankle (20), Retreat Right, Squat, Defend Ankle and Swirl (37), Thrust (38), Hit Temple, Close in and Rise (29), Kick Rib and Sit (30), Stand Up, Step Right and Thrust (31), Hit Right Temple (7), Step Left and Hit Temple (14), Step Right and Hit Three (15), Step Left and Defend Abdomen (16), Step Right and Thrust (11).

Second Series

Lean with a Long Step (32), Swing Right Outward, Stand Astride and Spring (33), Retreat Left and Right, Defend Thrust, Squat and Defend Ankle (34), Stand Up (90), Step Right and Hit Ankle (20), Step Left and Hit Right Temple (35), Retreat Left and Defend Head (36), Retreat Right and Defend Head (19), Step Right and Hit Ankle (20), Retreat Right, Squat, Defend Ankle and Swirl(37), Thrust

(38), Hit Right Temple squatting (39), Stand Up and Hit Temple (40), Step Right and Hit Three (15), Step Left and Defend Abdomen (16), Step Right and Thrust (11), Step Left and Hit Ankle (17), Hit Head by Right (18), Defend Abdomen, Spring Up, Squat and Defend Ankle (2), Rise Up and Hit Right Temple (3).

B. *Repeat Phases under* **F, G, H** *and* **I** *in the First Series.*

Third Series

A. Crouch with the Left Foot in Front (41), Retreat Crouching (42), Kick Right and Crouch (43), Kick Left High, Step and Leap (45).

B. Retreat and Hit Leg (46), Retreat Right, Stand Astride and Jump (47).

(A and B above together is called Prelude')

C. *Step Righty, Defend Temple, Jump and Turn (48), Step Right and Left, Turn and Hit Ankles (49), Retreat Left and Defend Head (36), Retreat Right and Defend Head (19), Step Right and Hit Ankle (20).* Retreat Right, Squat, Defend Ankle and Swirl (37), Thrust (38), Hit Right Temple squatting (39), Stand Up and Hit Temple (40), Step Right and Hit Three (15), Step Left and Defend Abdomen (16), Step Right and Thrust (11), Step Left and Hit Ankle (17), Hit Head by Right (18), Retreat Right and Crouch (50), Step Right, Defend Temple, Turn and Hit Ankles (51), Lean with a Long Step (32).

D. *Repeat the Phases in C which are in italics.*

E. Retreat Right and Defend Ankle (21), Defend Abdomen (22), Defend Abdomen and Chest (23 three times), Defend Hit with Right in Front (24), Thrust (right leading) (6), Hit Right Temple (7), Plant Baton and Defend Ankle (25), Hit Temple with Right Foot in Front (26), Hit Right Temple (7), Step Left, Defend Abdomen and Hit Right Temple (27), Step Right, Defend Abdomen and Hit Right Temple, Step Left and Hit Ankle (17), Retreat Left and Defend Head (36), Retreat Right and Defend Ankle (21), Hit Head by Right (18), Retreat Right and Crouch (50), Step Right, Defend Temple, Turn and Hit Ankles (51).

F. Retreat Left and Defend Head (36), Retreat Right and Defend Head (19), Step Right and Hit Ankle (20), Retreat Right, Squat, Defend Ankle and Swirl (37), Thrust (38), Hit Temple, Close in and Rise (29), Kick Rib and Sit (30), Stand Up, Step Right and Thrust (31), Hit Right Temple (7), Step Left and Hit Temple (14), Step Right and Hit Three (15), Step Left and Defend Abdomen (16), Step Right and Thrust (11).

Fourth Series

A. *Repeat Phases under A in the Third Series.*

B. Retreat and Hit Temple (52), Retreat Right, Stand Astride and Jump (47), Straight Right and Sit (53), Straight Left and Sit (54), Outward Right (55), Outward Left (56), Outward Right (55), Squat and Hit Ankle (57), Rise Up and Hit Right Temple (3), Retreat, Jump and Turn (58), Slide Right, Scissors Kick and Lean (59).

(A and B above together is called' Prelude')

C. *Step Right, Receive Hit and Ward Off (60), Step Forward and Thrust (61), Retreat Left and Defend Chest (62), Retreat Right and Crouch (50), Step Right, Defend Temple, Jump, Turn and Hit Ankles (63), Turn and Hit Ankles (64), Step Right, Defend Temple, Jump, Turn and Hit Ankles (63), Turn and Hit Ankles (64), Retreat Left and Defend Head (36), Retreat Right and Defend Head (19), Step Right and Hit Ankle (20),* Retreat Right, Squat, Defend Ankle and Swirl (37), Thrust (38), Hit Right Temple squatting (39), Stand Up and Hit Temple (40), Step Right and Hit Three (15), Step Left and Defend Abdomen (16), Step Right and Thrust (11), Step Left and Hit Ankle (17), Hit Head by Right (18), Retreat Right and Crouch (50), Step Right, Defend Temple, Turn and Hit Ankles (51), Lean with a Long Step (32).

D. *Repeat the Phases in C which are in italics.*

E. *Repeat Phases under E in the Third Series.*

F. *Repeat Phases under F in the Third Series.*

Fifth Series

A. *Repeat Phases under A in the Third Series.*

B. Retreat and Hit Temple (52), Retreat Right, Stand Astride and Jump (47), Straight Right and Sit (53), Straight Left and Sit (54), Outward Right (55), Outward Left (56), Outward Right (55), Squat, Defend Ankle and Swirl (65), Hit Thrice Squatting (66), Rise Up and Hit Right Temple (3), Retreat, Jump and Turn (58), Slide Right, Scissors Kick and Lean (59).

(A and B above together is called' Prelude')

C. *Defend Chest Retreating Twice (67), Defend Ankle and Swirl (76), Defend Head, jump and Defend Chest (68), Retreat Left and Swing Up Baton (69), Retreat Right and Crouch (50), Step Right, Defend Temple, Jump, Turn and Hit Ankles (63), Turn and Hit Ankles (64), Step Right, Defend Temple, Jump, Turn and Hit Ankles (63), Turn and Hit Ankles (64), Retreat Left and Defend Head (36), Retreat Right and Defend Head (19), Step Right and Hit Ankle (20),* Retreat Right, Squat, Defend Ankle and Swirl (37), Thrust (38), Hit Right Temple squatting (39), Stand Up and Hit Temple (40), Step Right and Hit Three (15), Step Left and Defend Abdomen (16), Step Right and Thrust (11), Step Left and Hit Ankle (17), Hit Head by Right (18), Retreat Right and Crouch (50), Step Right, Defend Temple, Turn and Hit Ankles (51), Lean with a Long Step (32).

D. *Repeat the Phases in C which are in italics.*

E. *Repeat Phases under E in the Third Series.*

F. *Repeat Phases under F in the Third Series.*

Sixth Series

A. *Repeat Phases under A in the Third Series.*

B. Retreat and Hit Temple (52), Retreat, Jump and Sit Back (70), Straight Left and Sit (54), Outward Right (55), Outward Left (56), Outward Right, Sit Sideways and Repeat (71), Squat and Hit Ankle (57), Hit Thrice Squatting (66), Squat, Defend Ankle and Swirl (65), Rise Up and Hit Right Temple (3), Withdraw Turning (72), Step Right and Left and Cross Batons (73), Retreat, Jump and Turn (58), Slide Right, Scissors Kick and Lean (59).

(A and B above together is called' Prelude')

C. *Step Right, Receive Hit and Ward Off (60), Step Left and Thrust Deep (74), Retreat left and Swing Up Baton (69), Retreat and Rotate Baton (75), Retreat Left and Defend Chest (62), Retreat Right and Crouch (50), Step Right, Defend Temple, Jump, Turn and Hit Ankles (63), Turn and Hit Ankles (64), Step Right, Defend Temple, Jump, Turn and Hit Ankles (63), Turn and Hit Ankles (64), Retreat left and Defend Head (36), Retreat Right and Defend Head (19), Step Right and Hit Ankle (20),* Retreat Right, Squat, Defend Ankle and Swirl (37), Thrust (38), Hit Right Temple squatting (39), Stand Up and Hit Temple (40), Step Right and Hit Three (15), Step Left and Defend Abdomen (16), Step Right and Thrust (11), Step Left and Hit Ankle (17), Hit Head by Right (18), Retreat Right and Crouch (50), Step Right, Defend Temple, Turn and Hit Ankles (51), Lean with a Long Step (32).

D. *Repeat the Phases in C which are in italics.*

E. *Repeat Phases under E in the Third Series.*

F. *Repeat Phases under F in the Third Series.*

Seventh Series

A. *Repeat A of the Sixth Series.*

B. *Repeat B of the Sixth Series.*

(A and B above together is called' Prelude')

C. *Defend Chest Retreating Twice (67), Defend Ankle and Swirl (76), Defend Head, Jump and Defend Chest*

(68), Retreat Left and Swing Up Baton (69), Retreat Right and Crouch (50), Step Right, Defend Temple, Jump, Turn and Hit Ankles (63), Turn and Hit Ankles (64), Step Right, Defend Temple, Jump, Turn and Hit Ankles (63), Turn, Hit Ankles and Swirl (77), Defend Head, Jump and Defend Chest (68), Retreat Left and Defend Head (36), Retreat Right and Defend Head (19), Step Right and Hit Ankle (20), Retreat Right, Squat, Defend Ankle and Swirl (37), Thrust (38), Hit Right Temple squatting (39), Stand Up and Hit Temple (40), Step Right and Hit Three (15), Step Left and Defend Abdomen (16), Step Right and Thrust (11), Step Left and Hit Ankle (17), Hit Head by Right (18), Retreat Right and Crouch (50), Step Right, Defend Temple, Turn and Hit Ankles (51), Lean with a Long Step (32).

D. *Repeat the Phases in C which are in italics.*

E. *Repeat Phases under E in the Third Series.*

F. Retreat Left and Defend Head (36), Retreat Right and Defend Head (19), Step Right and Hit Ankle (20), Retreat Right, Squat, Defend Ankle and Swirl (37), Stand Up, Jump and Hit Temples (78), Squat, Defend Ankle and Swirl (65), Thrust (38), Hit Temple, Close in and Rise (29), Kick Rib and Sit (30), Stand Up, Step Right and Thrust (31), Hit Right Temple (7), Step Left and Hit Temple (14), Step Right and Hit Three (15), Step Left and Defend Abdomen, Step Right and Thrust (11).

Eighth Series

A. *Repeat A of the Sixth Series.*

B. *Repeat B of the Sixth Series.*

(A and B above together is called' Prelude')

C. *Step Right, Receive Hit and Ward Off (60), Step Left and Thrust Deep (74), Retreat Left and Swing Up Baton (69), Retreat Right and Close In Chest (79), Retreat Left and Defend Ankle (80), Retreat Right and Crouch (50), Step Right, Defend Temple, Jump, Turn and Hit Ankles (63), Turn and Hit Ankles (64), Step Right, Defend Temple, Jump, Turn and Hit Ankles (63), Turn and Hit Ankles (64), Retreat Left and Defend Head (36), Retreat Right and Defend Head (19), Step Right and Hit Ankle (20),* Retreat Right, Squat, Defend Ankle and Swirl (37), Thrust (38), Hit Right Temple squatting (39), Stand Up and Hit Temple (40), Step Right and Hit Three (15), Step Left and Defend Abdomen (16), Step Right and Thrust (11), Step Left and Hit Ankle (17), Hit Head by Right (18), Retreat Right and Crouch (50), Step Right, Defend Temple, Turn and Hit Ankles (51), Lean with a Long Step (32).

D. *Repeat the Phases in C which are in italics.*

E. *Repeat Phases under E in the Third Series.*

F. Retreat Left and Defend Head (36), Retreat Right and Defend Head (19), Step Right and Hit Ankle (20), Retreat Right, Squat, Defend Ankle and Swirl (37), Defend Head and Ward Off (81), Thrust (38), Hit Temple, Close in and Rise (29), Kick Rib and Sit (30), Stand Up, Step Right and Thrust (31), Hit Right Temple (7), Step Left and Hit Temple (14), Step Right and Hit Three (15), Step Left and Defend Abdomen (16), Step Right and Thrust (11).

Ninth Series

A. *Repeat A of the Sixth Series.*

B. *Repeat B of the Sixth Series.*

(A and B above together is called' Prelude')

C. *Defend Chest Retreating Twice (67), Defend Ankle and Swirl (,76), Defend Head, Jump and Defend Chest (68), Retreat Left and Swing Up Baton (69), Retreat Right and Crouch (50), Step Right, Defend Temple, Jump, Turn and Hit Ankles (63), Turn and Hit Ankles (64), Squat (85), Thrust (38), Press Down Baton (82), Stand Up (90), Step Right, Defend Temple, Jump, Turn and Hit Ankles (63), Turn, Hit Ankles and Swirl (77), Defend Head, Jump and Defend Chest (68), Retreat Left and Defend Head (36), Retreat Right and Defend Head*

(19), Step Right and Hit Ankle (20), Retreat Right, Squat, Defend Ankle and Swirl (37), Thrust (38), Hit Right Temple squatting (39), Stand Up and Hit Temple (40), Step Right and Hit Three (15), Step Left and Defend Abdomen (16), Step Right and Thrust (11), Step Left and Hit Ankle (17), Hit Head by Right (18), Retreat Right and Crouch (50), Step Right, Defend Temple, Turn and Hit Ankles (51), Lean with a Long Step (32).

D. *Repeat the Phases in C which are in italics.*

E. *Repeat Phases under E in the Third Series.*

F. Retreat Left and Defend Head (36), Retreat Right and Defend Head (19), Step Right and Hit Ankle (20), Retreat Right, Squat, Defend Ankle and Swirl (37), Stand Up, Jump and Hit Temples (78), Squat, Defend Ankle and Swirl (65), Defend Head and Ward Off (81), Thrust (38), Hit Temple, Close in and Rise (29), Kick Rib and Sit (30), Stand Up, Step Right and Thrust (31), Hit Right Temple (7), Step Left and Hit Temple (14), Step Right and Hit Three (15), Step Left and Defend Abdomen (16), Step Right and Thrust (11).

EXERCISES WITH SHARP WEAPONS (*Angathaari*)

The ancient preceptors of India, including Varahamihira, Usanas and Kautilya, have elucidated the shapes and structures of a wide variety of weapons. They have also explained the scientific methods of tempering the metals used for making such weapons. These details do not come within the scope of this book.

The sharp weapons used in *angathaari* include swords and spears. Many of the exercises mastered in *maippayattu* and *kolethaari* are constantly used in *angathaari*.

To avert possible injury, you should first practise the exercises to perfection with blunt weapons like cane or bamboo batons and only then begin to practise with the sharp weapons.

Swinging Exercises with the Sword and Shield (*Valvali*)

The series of exercises in *valvali* help one to master the techniques employed in wielding the sword and shield. They are practised by an individual in mock attacks aimed at imaginary opponents.

The sword used here is about three feet long from the hilt to the tip. The shield, made of copper, steel or zinc is about one-and-a-half feet in diameter.

Valvali is done in two different styles. In one the student wields the sword very close to his body with agile grace and is meant to exhibit his mastery of this weapon. In the other, while almost all the exercises are similar to those in the earlier one, the student executes forceful cuts and thrusts with the sword as if attacking an opponent.

PHASES EXPLAINED

Phase I - GUARD CHEST

- Standing with the left step in front, slightly leaning forward, hold the shield guarding the chest. The sword should be held in the right hand on the right side, at waist line, the tip pointing slightly downward.

Phase 2 - WHIRL SWORD, STEP RIGHT AND CUT NECK

- Whirl the sword anti-clockwise, vertically, close to your body on the right side, by rotating your wrist. The grip on the sword should be at chest level.
- Step right foot forward and without breaking the flow of the sword, swing it overhead anti-clockwise and execute a cut at the right side of the opponent's neck in front.

Phase 3 - STEP LEFT AND CROUCH

- Step forward with the left, bring the sword to the right side of the body and assume a 'crouch' posture. Lift the shield overhead and then bring it down to guard the chest while crouching.

Phase 4 - WHIRL SWORD, TURN AND RETREAT

- Rise up and whirl the sword clockwise, vertically, close to your body on the right side, by rotating your wrist.
- Turn by the right to the opposite direction and step forward with the left foot pointing the sword horizontally forward at chest level, the sharp edge turned upward. In continuation, turn by the right to the original direction and step right foot backwards.
- While doing this the sword should be swung neck level, from left to right, arm stretched.

Phase 5 - STEP RIGHT AND PROTECT CHEST

- Step forward with the right foot and bring the sword and shield in front of the chest, the fists touching each other. The tip of the sword should be pointing backwards, blunt side of the blade resting on the right upper arm.

Phase 6 - STEP LEFT AND PROTECT HEAD

- Step forward with a long left, and lift the shield overhead slightly to the front, arm stretched. Hold the sword at right waist line close to the body, tip pointing forward.

Phase 7 - RETREAT LEFT AND CUT ANKLE

- Step backwards with the left foot and crouch.
- While stepping back, swing the sword from the right to the left close to the floor as if to cut at the ankle of the opponent in front. Simultaneously, hold the shield overhead, slightly to the front and look up at it.

Phase 8 - SLASH ABDOMEN

- Raising from the 'crouch' posture, holding the shield covering the chest bring the sword (the tip turned downward) vertically in front of the shield, the sharp edge turned outward.
- Then swing the sword upward as if to slash along the abdomen up to the forehead of the opponent in front.

Phase 9 - CUT HEAD

- Swing down the sword as if to cut at the head of the opponent in front.

Phase 10 - STEP LEFT AND THRUST

- Withdraw the sword towards the right waist-line.
- Then lunge forward with the left foot, stretching both arms fully with fists close together, thrust with the point of the sword at the abdomen of the opponent in front.

Phase 11 - WITHDRAW LEFT AND SLASH ABDOMEN

- Step backwards with the left foot bringing both the sword and shield in front of the chest, sword held vertically in front of the shield, the tip pointing downwards, the sharp edge turned outward.
- Continuing, swing the sword upward as if to slash vertically along the abdomen up to the forehead of the opponent in front, simultaneously raising the shield overhead.

Phase 12 - TURN TO LEFT AND CROUCH

- Turn to the left and stand astride, feet a shoulder width apart, and crouch. Hold the shield guarding the chest. Hold the sword at your right knee-level.

Phase 13 - CUT NECK, SLASH ABDOMEN AND STAND UP

- Move sword in an arc-wise manner from right to the left as if to cut at the neck of the opponent, cross the forearms, right over the left, the tip of the sword pointing left downward.
- Return the sword in an arc-wise manner from left to right to cut at the right side of the opponent's neck.
- Lift the shield overhead as if to defend a hit on the head.
- Slash the sword upwards as if to cut the abdomen of the opponent. Simultaneously, rise up and bring down the shield to protect your chest.

Phase 14 - TURN HALF CIRCLE AND RIP CHEST

- Stretching the arm, swing the sword from left to right at chest level and turn by the right to the opposite direction moving the right foot and stand astride.

Phase 15 - WEAVE SWORD AROUND NECK, TURN RIGHT, LUNGE LEFT AND THRUST

- Without breaking the flow of the sword, bend the right arm so as to place the blunt edge of the blade on the right shoulder, tip pointing backwards.
- Then move the hilt from the right to the left around the back of the neck.
- Simultaneously turning to the right withdraw the weapons to the waist-line on either side of the body and thrust the weapons stretching the arms forward, lunging with the left foot with a long step.

Phase 16 - TURN QUARTER CIRCLE TO RIGHT AND RIP CHEST

- Swing the sword at neck level stretching the arm, from the left to the right, and turn to the right and assume the starting position by withdrawing the right foot.

Phase 17 - SWING AND CUT THRICE

- With the left foot leading, aim a cut from the right at the left temple of the opponent in front.
- Then continuing the movement of the sword, execute a cut on the head from the left side.
- And then swinging the sword in an anti-clockwise manner above the head horizontally deliver a cut on the right side of the opponent's neck. (All these should be done in a single flowing motion.)

Phase 18 - STEP RIGHT FORWARD AND BACKWARD, SWING, CUT THRICE AND CROUCH

- Stepping forward with the right, execute these same three cuts (as in Phase 17).
- But while executing the third cut, i.e. on the right side of the neck, step back the right foot. While stepping back, lift the shield overhead and bring it down to guard the chest, and assume the 'crouch' posture. The sword should be held on the right side.

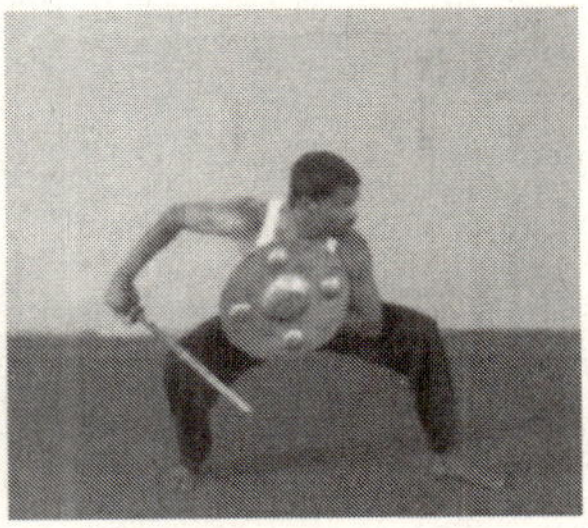

Phase 19 - WEAVE SWORD AROUND NECK, TURN ONE-AND-A-QUARTER CIRCLE, LUNGE LEFT AND THRUST

- Without breaking the flow of the sword, bend the right arm so as to place the blunt edge of the blade on the right shoulder, tip pointing backwards.
- Move the sword from the right shoulder to the left shoulder through the back of the neck and continue to weave the sword around the neck once more in succession.
- While doing this turn the body clockwise one and a quarter circle once. Move the left foot through the front towards the right and step aside turning by the right to the opposite direction (half circle). In succession, move the right foot by the rear towards the left and step aside turning by the right to the opposite direction (half circle).

- Then withdraw the weapons to the waist-line on either side of the body, turn quarter circle by the right and thrust the weapons stretching the arms forward, lunging with the left foot with a long step. (Take care to syncronize the movements of the feet, body and weapons so as to give grace and unbroken continuity to this phase.)

Phase 20 - MOVE SWORD BACK ALONG RIBS, TURN ONE AND A QUARTER CIRCLE, LUNGE LEFT AND THRUST

- Without breaking the flow of the sword, bend the right arm so as to place the blunt side of the blade on the right shoulder, tip pointing backwards.
- Move the hilt from the right to left around the back of the neck and without breaking the flow of the sword, bring the sword in front of the chest, tip pointing upward. Lifting the right elbow sideways, turn the blade anti-clockwise to bring the tip pointing downward, the sharp edge facing outward, the hilt at chest level.
- Then move the blade on to the back of the body along the right ribs under the right armpit, and hold it vertically on the back along the spine, blunt edge touching the body, the tip pointing upwards.
- Then reverse the movement to bring the sword in front of the chest, turn the blade clockwise, tip pointing upwards.
- Move the grip around the back of the neck from the right to left and bring the sword in front.
- While performing these sword movements, move the right foot through the rear to the left and step aside turning by the right to the opposite direction (half circle). In succession, move the left foot by the front towards the right and step aside, turning by the right to the opposite direction (half circle).
- Then withdraw the weapons to the waist line on either side of the body, turn quarter circle by the right and thrust the weapons stretching the arms forward lunging with the left foot with a long step.
  (Take care to syncronize the movements of the feet, body and weapons so as to give grace and unbroken continuity to this phase.)

Phase 21 - WHIRL SWORD, SCISSORS KICK AND TURN RIGHT

- With the left foot leading, whirl the sword vertically on the right side, anti-clockwise, rotating the wrist.
- Step forward with the right foot and execute a scissors kick to the front and land on the left and turn to the right to stand astride.
- While executing the scissors kick, swing the sword overhead from the left to the right stretching the arm.

ORAL COMMANDS

Salutation

Guard Chest (Phase 1), Whirl Sword, Step Right and Cut Neck (Phase 2), Step Left and Crouch (Phase 3), Whirl Sword, Turn and Retreat (Phase 4), Step Right and Protect Chest (Phase 5)

First Series

A. Step Left and Protect Head (6), Retreat Left and Cut Ankle (7), Slash Abdomen (8), Cut Head (9), Step Left and Thrust (10), Withdraw Left and Slash Abdomen (11), Turn to Left and Crouch (12), Cut Neck, Slash Abdomen and Stand Up (13), Turn Half Circle and Rip Chest (14).

B. Weave Sword around Neck, Turn Right, Lunge Left and Thrust (15).

C. Withdraw Left and Slash Abdomen (11), Turn to Left and Crouch (12), Cut Neck, Slash Abdomen and Stand Up (13), Turn Half Circle and Rip Chest (14).

D. Weave Sword around Neck, Turn Right, Lunge Left and Thrust (15).

E. Withdraw Left and Slash Abdomen (11), Turn to Left and Crouch (12), Cut Neck, Slash Abdomen and Stand Up (13), Turn quarter circle and Rip Chest (16), Swing and Cut Thrice (17), Step Right Forward and Backward, Swing, Cut Thrice and Crouch (18).

Second Series

Repeat all the Phases under A, C and E in the First Series; instead of Phase 15 (B and D) in the First Series, do Weave Sword around Neck, Turn One and Quarter Circle, Lunge Left and Thrust (19).

Third Series

Repeat all the Phases under A, C and E in the First Series; instead of Phase 15 (B and D) in the First Series, do Move Sword back along Ribs, Turn One and Quarter Circle, Lunge Left and Thrust (20).

Fourth Series

A. Step Left and Protect Head (6), Retreat Left and Cut Ankle (7), Slash Abdomen (8), Cut Head (9), Step Left and Thrust (10), Withdraw Left and Slash Abdomen (11), Turn to Left and Crouch (12), Cut Neck, Slash Abdomen and Stand Up (13), Turn Quarter Circle and Rip Chest (16).

B. Whirl Sword, Scissors Kick and Turn Right (21), Move Sword Back along Ribs, Turn One and Quarter Circle, Lunge Left and Thrust (20).

C. Withdraw Left and Slash Abdomen (11), Turn to Left and Crouch (12), Cut Neck, Slash Abdomen and Stand Up (13), Turn Quarter Circle and Rip Chest (16).

D. Whirl Sword, Scissors Kick and Turn Right (21), Move Sword Back along Ribs, Turn One and Quarter Circle, Lunge Left and Thrust (20).

E. Withdraw Left and Slash Abdomen (11), Turn to Left and Crouch (12), Cut Neck, Slash Abdomen and Stand Up (13), Turn Quarter Circle and Rip Chest (16), Swing and Cut thrice (17), Step Right forward and backward, Swing, Cut thrice and Crouch (18).

Exercises with the Sword and Shield (*Valppayattu*)

The sword was considered the most lethal of all weapons used by combatants of yore all over the world. And it was glorified to symbolise valour, power and justice.

There are some who hold the view that the dagger, which was once the most popular as a handy weapon, was eventually transformed into the long-bladed sword. In Indian and overseas literature, we find mention of a wide variety of daggers and swords of different lengths and shapes.

Churika, which is a special kind of sword, was an important weapon used by the stalwarts of *payattu.* The ballads of North Malabar are replete with stories of swordsmen wielding the *churika* in duels. In the volume entitled *KALARI VIDYA,* the *vaaithaari* of *churika payattu* is given, but none now appears to know how to practise the exercises with the *churika.*

In palm leaf manuscripts and ballads we read of the many extraordinary feats of the swordsmen of yore. The old masters of *kalarippayattu* retained many of the exercises of *valppayattu* by teaching them to succeeding generations.

In *kalarippayattu*, *valppayattu* denotes the exercises where two athletes wield a sword and a shield. The sword and shield used here are identical to those used in *valvali* and there are well-regulated techniques of defence and attack.

PHASES EXPLAINED

- ❑ *Done inside a kalari, M and P stand in the West and East in the middle of the kalari facing each other about ten feet away while starting these exercises.*
- ❑ *The one with the white wrist bands is M, the other is P.*

Phase I - GUARD CHEST

Action P and M

- Stand facing each other about ten feet away.
- With the left foot in front, lean body forward a little, hold the shield close to the body in front guarding your chest. The sword, in the right hand, is held at your right waist line, the tip of the sword pointing forward.

Phase 2 - SWING WEAPONS AND BOW

Action P and M

- Swing the sword clockwise in a vertical plane on your left side, simultaneously swinging the shield anti-clockwise on your right side, the right arm over the left. And then stretch arms overhead holding the sword and shield close to each other.

- In continuation, bring the weapons down to hold them in front of your chest, the forearms held pressed close to each other vertically. Here, the blunt edge of the blade should rest on the right upper arm, tip of the sword pointing backwards.
- From there, lower the body by stretching the right leg backwards with a long step, and bring the sword and shield down to press on the floor.
- Stand up and face each other as at the start of this Phase.

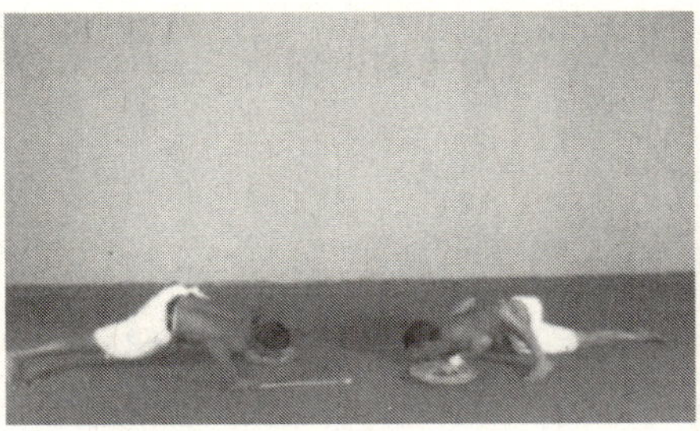

Phase 3 - STEP LEFT, TROT, SQUAT AND SWING WEAPONS

Action P and M

- Stand facing each other as in Phase I.
- Kick in front with your left foot, and then step forward with that foot.
- Take off on your left foot and trot forward. Then assume a 'squat' posture, with your right foot in the rear.
- While trotting forward and squatting, swing your weapons on both sides of your body as in Phase 2.
- Remaining in the 'squat' posture, aim a cut with the sword from the right at the left temple of the opponent in front. Then continuing the movement of the sword, execute a cut on the head from the left side. And then swinging the sword in an anti-clockwise manner overhead horizontally deliver a cut on the right side of the opponent's neck.
- After the last cut at the right side of the neck, lift the shield overhead and bring it down to guard the chest.

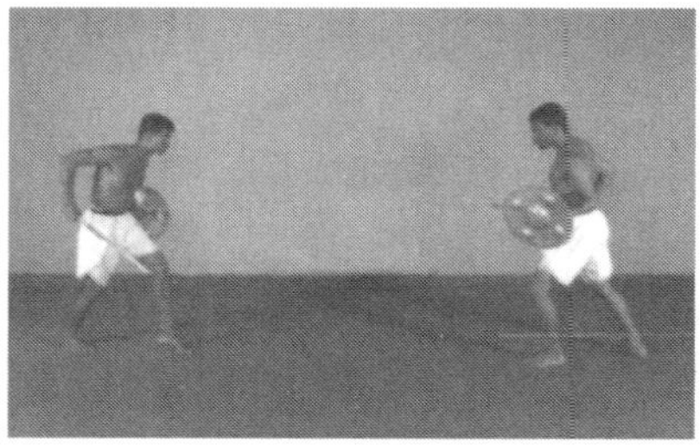

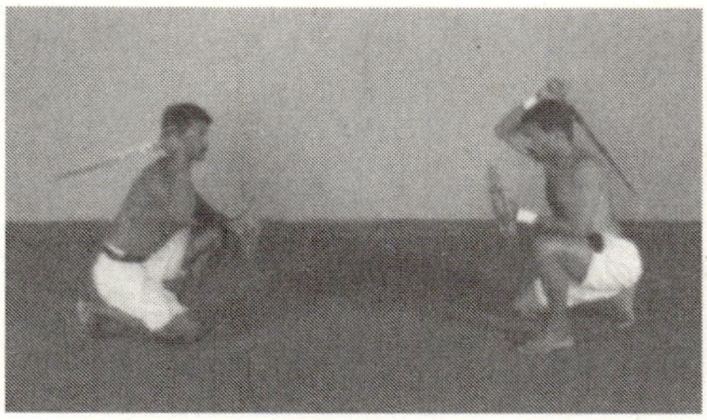

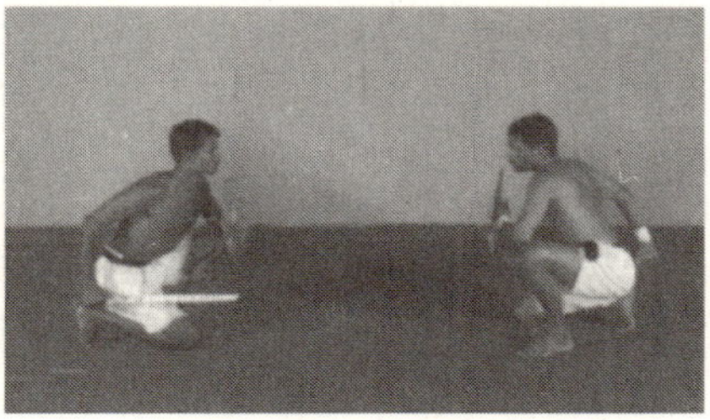

Phase 4 - RISE UP, RETREAT, JUMP AND TURN

Action P and M

- Rise up.
- Turn by the right to the opposite direction and point the sword forward, hand held supine.
- Take off on the right foot and jump forward to land on the left. Simultaneously, turn to the opposite direction by the right and move your right foot through the rear and keep it behind. While turning swing the sword overhead in an anti-clockwise manner in a horizontal plane. Then stand facing each other with the left foot leading.
- The 'Jump and Turn' should be done in such a way that the body is air-born horizontally. The legs should be in a folded position, the feet remaining straight.

Phase 5 - SWING SWORD, TURN AND CROUCH

Action P and M

- Remaining with the left foot in front, swing three cuts, one each at the left temple of the opponent, head and the right side of the neck without breaking the flow of the sword.
- Then stepping forward with the right foot, aim a cut at the left side of the opponent's neck and turn full circle by the left to face each other and crouch with the right foot in the rear. Defend this cut with your sword meeting the attack mid-way.

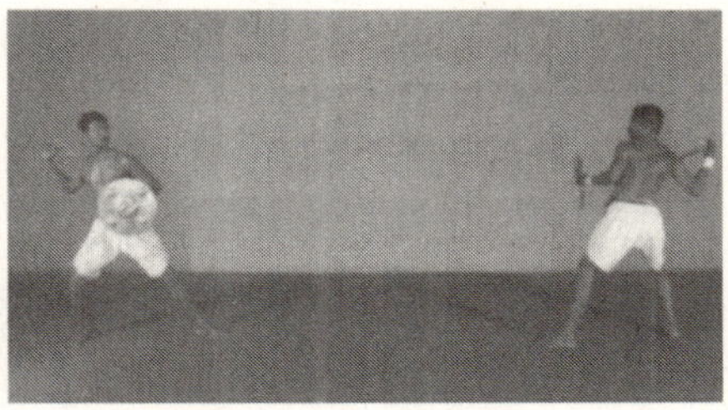

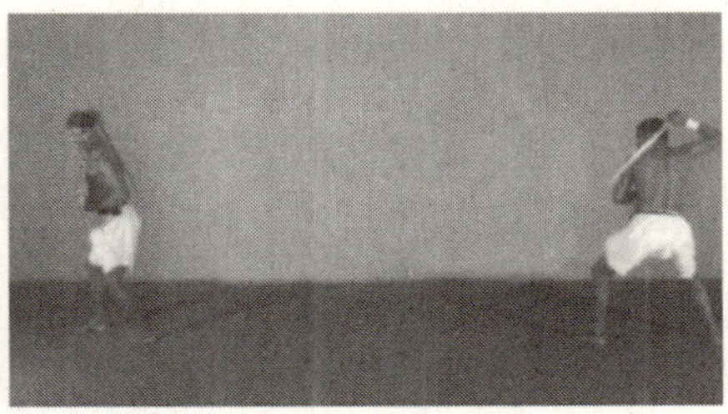

Phase 6 - STAND UP, KICK LEFT, TROT AND CUT THREE

Action P and M

- Stand up and kick in front with the left and step forward.
- Take off on the left and trot forward.
- Then execute three separate cuts in succession, first at the right side of the neck, crossing forearms, right over left, then left side of the neck uncrossing forearms, and again right side of the neck of the opponent crossing forearms.
- Simultaneously, defend cuts of the opponent with the shield moving it on either side of the neck.

Phase 7 - RETREAT, JUMP AND TURN

Action P and M

- Repeat 'Retreat, Jump and Turn' as in Phase 4.

Phase 8 - STEP FORWARD, CLASH, JUMP AND TURN

Action P and M

- Stand up and cross the weapons held close in front of the chest.
- With a long left step forward, clash at each other.
- Then stepping forward diagonally with a long right step to the left side, take off on it, jump forward and land on the left foot.
- Then turn by the right to the opposite direction to face each other with the right foot in the rear. Then execute a cut at each other's neck on the right side by swinging the sword. Simultaneously, defend the cut by moving the shield towards the right.

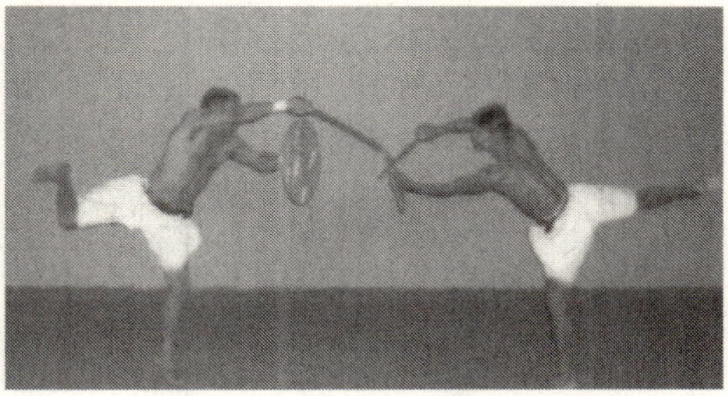

Phase 9 - CLASH, TURN AND CUT NECK

Action P and M

- Stand facing each other with the left foot in front.
- Move forward and clash the weapons against each other's, still with the left foot in front.
- Step forward with the right foot slightly to the left, pass each other by the right side.
- Then P and M simultaneously cut at each other's left neck and defend the cuts.
- Then cut at the opponent's left neck and defend cut from the opponent aimed at the left side of the neck simultaneously.
- Trot back and face each other with a long right step backward.

Phase 10 - DASH FORWARD AND CUT ANKLES

Action P and M

- Step apart ten feet away facing each other with the left foot in front.
- Dashing forward at each other and stepping forward with the right foot, swing the sword from the left to right and then right to left aiming cuts at each other's ankles. Here the swords should clash while defending the ankles.

Phase 11 - RETREAT RIGHT AND CLASH WEAPONS

Action P and M

- P stepping backwards with the right foot and M stepping forward with the left foot, holding the weapons crossed (sword in front of the shield) in front of the chest, thrust them forward to clash at each other in front.

Phase 12 - PIVOT AND THRUST

Action P and M

- Withdrawing the left foot and pivoting full circle on the right foot by the right and standing to face each other with the left foot in front, execute and defend thrusts at each other's left side of the lower abdomen.

Phase 13 - SWING TWO CUTS

Action P and M

- Remaining with the left foot in front, cut and defend at each other's right ribs, arms crossed right over the left.
- Then cut and defend each other's left ribs uncrossing the arms.

Phase 14 - CUT HEAD AND CIRCLE

Action P and M

- Step forward diagonally towards the left with the right and left foot.
- Simultaneously, swing the sword clockwise at the left side and anti-clockwise on the right side vertically close to the body.
- Move the right foot slightly towards the left in the rear to stand face to face with each other. Then without breaking the flow of the sword, execute a cut at each other's head. Simultaneously, defend the cut of each other by lifting the shield overhead.
- Repeat these movements four or five times by moving and coming to full circle.

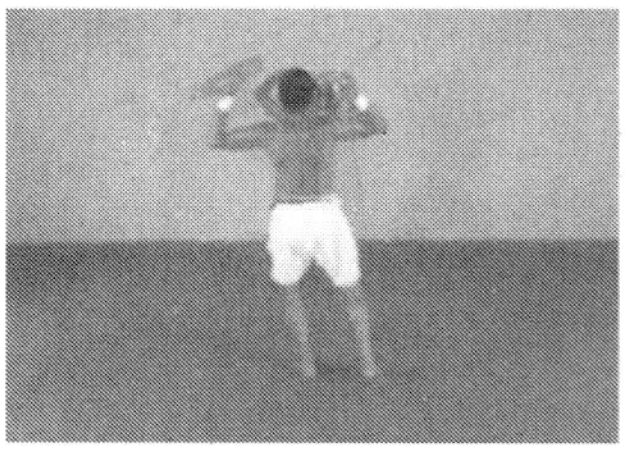
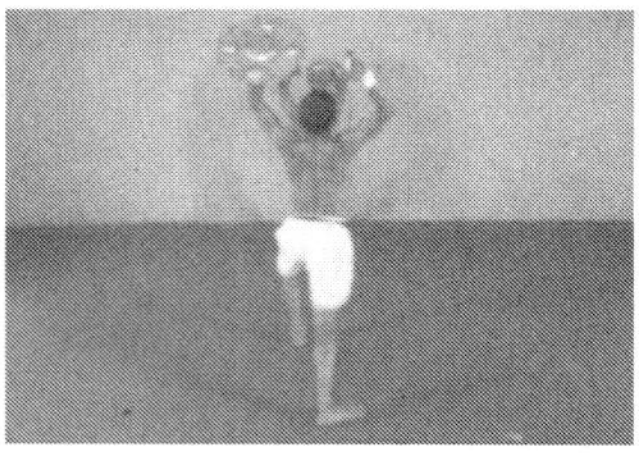

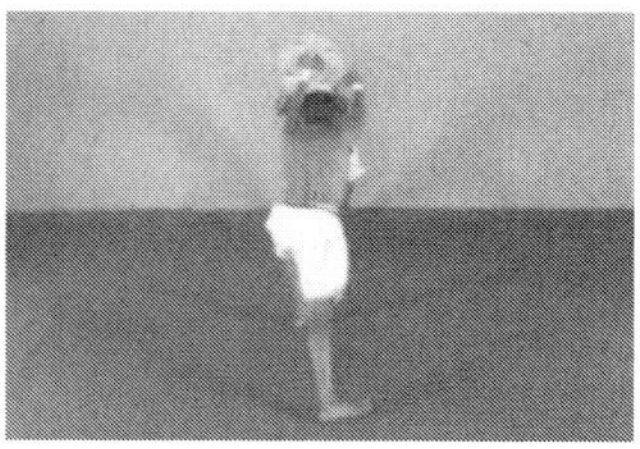

Phase 15 - STEP FORWARD AND CLOSE-IN CHEST

Action P and M

- Step forward with a long left step.
- Cut at each other's right temple, the two swords crossing midway.
- In this position, move the shield forward to close-in against each other, chest to chest, while pushing the weapons upwards to bring them overhead.

Phase 16 - CUT ANKLE, RETREAT AND TURN

Action P and M

- Withdrawing the left foot and separating from each other, cut at each other's right inner ankle with the sword.
- Then turning by the left full circle, remain with the right foot in the rear with a long step and face each other.

Phase 17 - DASH FORWARD AND CUT RIBS

Action P and M

- Dashing forward at each other and stepping forward with the left foot, first cut the left ribs, then crossing the arms cut the right ribs.
- Simultaneously, defend the opponent's cuts by moving the shield to the left and then to the right.

Phase 18 - TURN FULL CIRCLE AND CUT THRICE

Action P and M

- Withdrawing the left foot, pivot full circle on the right foot, by the right, and facing each other with the left foot in front, swing three cuts, first at the right ribs, then left ribs and again right ribs.
- Simultaneously, defend these cuts by moving the shield.

Phase 19 - JUMP UP AND CUT HEAD

Action P

- Stand astride. Spring up high to avoid M's cut aimed at the feet. While in mid-air, swing down a cut at M's head. Land and stand with your left foot in front.

Action M

- Dash forward with the left foot in front, swing the sword from the left to right horizontally with the blade almost touching the floor to cut at the feet of P. Lift the shield overhead to defend P's cut.

Phase 20 - PIERCE ABDOMEN

Action P

- Remaining with the left foot in front, thrust the sword forward to pierce M's abdomen.
- Then stepping forward with the right, thrust again to pierce at M's abdomen.

Action M

- Remaining with the left foot in front, thrust down P's attack with the shield.
- Stepping backwards with the left foot, thrust down again to defend the second attack as well.

Phase 21 - CUT RIGHT AND LEFT RIBS ADVANCING

Action P

- Stepping forward with the left and then with the right foot, aim two cuts, first at M's left ribs and then at right ribs. Simultaneously, defend M's cut with the shield at the left ribs and right ribs.

Action M

- Stepping backwards with the right and then left foot, cut and defend as P.

Phase 22 - CLASH AND PRESS

Action P and M

- P stepping backwards with the right foot and M stepping forward with the left foot, and holding the weapons crossed in front of the chest, thrust the weapons forward to clash them against each other's and hold them pressed at each other's.

Phase 23 - RETREAT AND CUT RIGHT TEMPLE

Action P and M

- P stepping backwards with the left foot and M stepping forward with the right foot, cut at each other's right temples with the sword.

Phase 24 - CUT ANKLE, SWING BODY BACKWARDS TURNING AND CUT RIBS

Action P and M

- Remaining with the right foot in front, cut at each other's right inner ankle and turning full circle by the left to face each other with the right foot in the rear. While turning around, the body should be bent backwards.
- Remaining with the left foot in front, aim two cuts, one at the right ribs and then left ribs. Simultaneously, defend cuts by moving the shield.

Phase 25 - CUT TEMPLES AND TURN

Action P and M

- Stepping forward diagonally with a long right step towards the left side, aim a cut at each other's left temple.
- Then pass each other by the right side, step diagonally forward with the left foot towards the right side, turn by the right to the opposite direction.
- Then keeping the right foot in the rear, aim a cut at each other's right temple.

Phase 26 - CUT WAIST-LINE AND TROT BACK

Action P and M

- Remaining with the left foot in front, trot back after cutting at each other's left waist-line.
- The trot should be timed so that the swords cross in front without allowing the cut to reach the target.

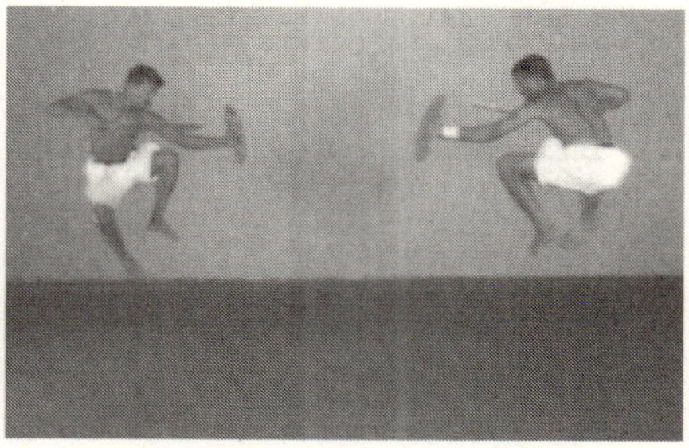

Phase 27 - LEAP HIGH TURNING AND CROUCH

Action P and M

- Stepping diagonally forward with the right foot to the left side, take off on it.
- Passing each other on the right side, land on the left foot by turning by the right to the opposite direction to stand facing each other.
- While air-borne and turning by the right, the body should be in a horizontal plane, the legs folded with the feet held straight.
- While in action, the sword should be swung from the left to right.
- After landing, stand facing each other in the 'crouch' posture.

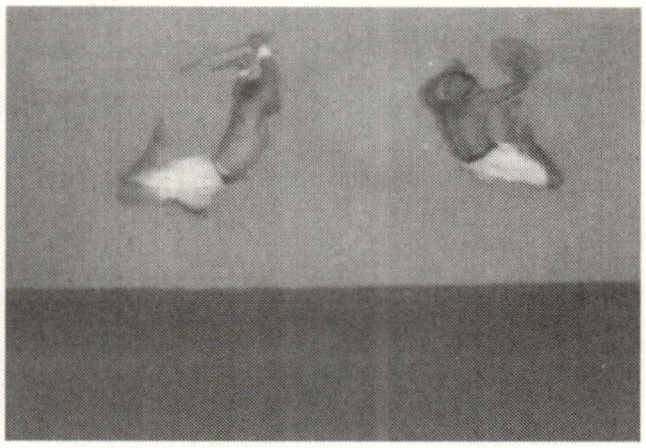

Phase 28 - DASH FORWARD AND RIP ABDOMEN

Action P and M

- Stand up, dash forward at each other, and with the right foot in front, rip from abdomen upwards to forehead simultaneously defending with the shield.

Phase 29 - TURN AND CLASH WEAPONS

Action P and M

- Step forward diagonally towards the left with a long right step and cut at each other's left temple with the sword.
- Then passing each other by the right side, step forward diagonally towards the right with a long left step and turn by the right to the opposite direction remaining with the right foot in the rear to face each other.
- While keeping the right foot in the rear thrust forward the weapons crossed in front of the chest and clash them against each other's.

Phase 30 - CUT AND DEFEND HEAD CIRCLING

Action P and M

- Repeat Phase 14. But instead of wielding the weapons held together while cutting and defending the head, here P executes a cut first which M defends with the shield, and then M executes a cut which P defends with his shield.
- This is repeated two or three times to complete half a circle

Phase 31 - STAND UP, ADVANCE, CUT RIBS AND ANKLES

Action P and M

- Stand up and advance towards each other.
- With the left foot in front, cut at the right and left ribs. Simultaneously, defend with the shield the cuts aimed at the right and left ribs.
- Thereafter, cut at the left outer and inner ankles in quick succession. Simultaneously, defend these cuts with the sword.

Phase 32 - CUT RIBS, HEAD AND WAIST-LINE ADVANCING

Action P and M

- P stepping forward with a long right step, and M stepping backwards with a long left step, both attack and defend each other's left ribs.
- Then P again stepping forward with a long left step, and M stepping backwards with a long right step, both attack and defend each other's right ribs, crossing arms.
- Again P stepping forward with a long right step and M stepping backwards with a long left step, attack and defend each other's head by lifting up the shield and swinging the sword downward.
- Again P stepping forward with a long left step and M stepping backwards with a long right step, attack and defend (with the sword and shield) each other's left waist-line.

ORAL COMMANDS

Salutation

Guard Chest (Phase 1), Swing Weapons and Bow (Phase 2), Step Left, Trot, Squat and Swing Weapons (Phase 3), Rise Up, Retreat, Jump and Turn (Phase 4)

First Series

Swing Sword, Turn and Crouch (5), Stand Up, Kick Left, Trot and Cut Three (6), Retreat, Jump and Turn (7), Step Forward, Slash, Jump and Turn (8), Clash, Turn and Cut Neck (9).

Second Series

Dash Forward and Cut Ankles (10), Retreat Right and Clash Weapons (11), Pivot and Thrust (12), Swing Two Cuts (13), Cut Head and Circle (14), Step Forward and Close in Chest (15), Cut Ankle, Retreat and Turn (16).

Third Series

A. Dash Forward and Cut Ribs (17), Turn Full Circle and Cut Thrice (18), Cut Ankle, Retreat and Turn (16), Jump and Cut Head (19), Pierce Abdomen (20), Cut Right and Left Ribs advancing (21), Clash and Press (22).

B. Pivot and Thrust (12), Retreat and Cut Right Temple (23), Cut Ankle, Swing Body Backwards turning and Cut Ribs (24), Cut Temples and Turn (25), Cut Waist line and Trot Back (26), Leap High turning and Crouch (27).

C. Dash Forward and Rip Abdomen (28), Turn and Clash Weapons (29), Cut and Defend Head circling (30), Clash and Press (22).

D. Pivot and Thrust (12), Retreat and Cut Right Temple (23), Cut Ankle, Swing Body Backwards turning and Cut Ribs (24), Cut Temples and Turn (25), Cut Waist line and Trot Back (26), Leap High turning and Crouch (27).

E. Stand Up, Advance, Cut Ribs and Ankles (31), Retreat and Cut Right Temple (23), Cut Ribs, Head and Waistline advancing (32).

Exercises with Sword-shield and Spear (*Mara Pitichu Kuntha Payattu*)

Unlike the other defence exercises in *kalarippayattu* practised in pairs with identical weapons, the exercises in *mara pitichu kuntha payattu* are done using different weapons. One (M) wields the sword and shield, while the other (P) wields the spear.

The spear used in *payattu* is a five-foot long cane or bamboo staff with a pointed spearhead attached to one end.

Even though the sword has the pride of place among weapons, the preceptors of *payattu* did not shy away from experimenting with other weapons to counter the sword. And a unique series of techniques of defence and attack with the spear pitched against a swordsman, were developed.

Depending upon the expertise of the one who wields it, the spear could effectively keep the swordsman at bay. The spearhead and the grip-end of the spear could be employed to pierce and hit.

There are regularised techniques of defence and attack using these weapons in *payattu*.

Fig. 1 gripping the spear

PHASES EXPLAINED

❑ *Done inside a kalari, M and P stand in the West and East in the middle of the kalari facing each other about ten feet away while starting these exercises.*

Phase I - ROTATE SPEARHEAD, STEP RIGHT AND HIT HEAD

Action P

- Stand with a long left step in front.
- Hold the spear as in Fig. I, pointing the spearhead towards M's chest, the weapon held on your right at the chest-level.
- Rotate the point of the spear in small circles in a clockwise direction.
- Then step forward with your right foot and hit M's head with the grip-end of the spear.

Action M

- Stand with left foot in front, facing P.
- Guard your chest with the shield held close to the chest and hold the sword on your right at waist-line.
- Stepping backwards with the left foot, lift the weapons overhead, a little ahead in front, and defend P's hit aimed at your head. The weapons should be crossed, the sword remaining over the shield, while receiving the hit.

Phase 2 - STEP LEFT AND PIERCE ABDOMEN

Action P

- While stepping forward with the left foot, move the spearhead from the left side of your body in an anti-clockwise direction, and pierce M's abdomen.

Action M

- While stepping backwards with the right foot, push down the spearhead with your weapons.

Phase 3 - TROT BACK AND CROUCH

Action P

- Trot backwards and stand with the left foot still in front. While trotting, swing the spearhead in an anti-clockwise direction on the left side of your body to aim a hit at M's abdomen with the grip-end of the spear from your right side.
- Again aim a hit at M's abdomen with the spearhead from your left side.
- While delivering these two hits, slide your grip on the spear appropriately and make it a flowing motion.

Action M

- Trot forward with the left foot still in front.
- Guard your chest and abdomen with the weapons held a little ahead. Adjust your pace so that P's attacks do not reach your weapons.

Phase 4 - STEP RIGHT AND HIT HEAD

Action P

- Step forward with a long right step and hit M's head with the grip-end of the spear.

Action M

- Step backwards with the left foot, lift the weapons crossed overhead a little ahead in front and thus defend P's hit aimed at your head.

Phase 5 - RETREAT RIGHT AND DEFEND ANKLE

Action P

- Step backwards with the right foot, swing the spearhead from your left side slanting down to the right and thus defend M's cut aimed at your left inner ankle.

Action M

- Step forward with the left foot and wield a cut at P's inner left ankle with the sword.

Phase 6 - HIT HEAD

Action P

- Remaining with the left foot in front, hit at M's head with the grip-end of the spear.

Action M

- Remaining with the left foot in front, lift the weapons crossed overhead and thus defend P's hit aimed at your head.

Phase 7 - RETREAT LEFT AND HIT HEAD

Action P

- Step backwards with the left foot and hit again at M's head with the grip-end by swinging the spear on the right side of your body in an anti-clockwise direction.

Action M

- Step forward with the right foot and defend P's hit on your head by lifting the weapons overhead crossed.

Phase 8 - STEP BACK AND PIERCE FOOT

Action P

- Step backwards with the right foot and pierce M's left foot, by bringing the spearhead from the left side of your body.

Action M

- Step forward with the left foot, swing the sword from the left diagonally downward and thus defend P's attack.

Phase 9 - HIT TEMPLE

Action P

- Remaining with the left foot in front, lift up the spearhead and with it hit at M's right temple.

Action M

- Remaining with the left foot in front, swing up the sword and thus defend P's hit aimed at your right temple.

Phase 10 - STEP RIGHT AND LEFT AND PIERCE

Action P

- Step forward with the right foot and aim a hit at M's lower abdomen by swinging up the grip-end of the spear.
- Then step forward with the left foot and pierce M's chest with the spearhead.
- While doing these, your hands gripping the spear should be moved as if reverse pedalling a bicycle.

Action M

- Step backwards with the left and avert the hit aimed at your abdomen. Then step back with the right foot and deflect P's attack with the spearhead by ducking down a little and by lifting your weapons upwards.
- While stepping backwards, swirl the sword on the right side of your body in a vertical plane, anti-clockwise, by rotating your wrist.

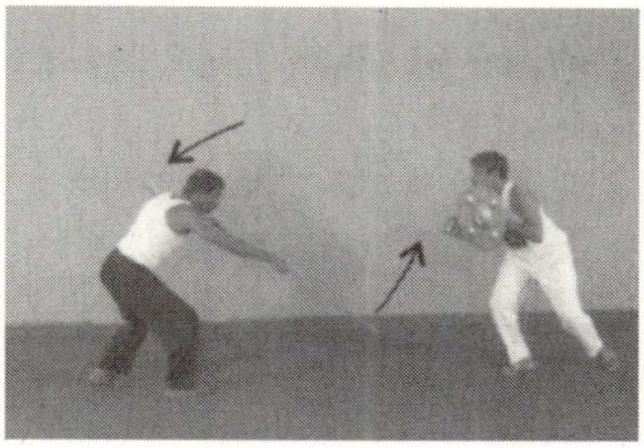

Phase 11 - RETREAT LEFT AND DEFEND ANKLE

Action P

- Step backwards with the left foot and defend M's cut aimed at your right inner ankle, with the grip-end of the spear.

Action M

- Step forward with the right foot and aim to cut P's right inner ankle with the sword.

Phase 12 - RETREAT RIGHT AND HIT TEMPLE

Action P

- Step backwards with the right foot.
- Simultaneously, swing the grip-end of the spear in an anti-clockwise direction on the right side of your body and hit at M's left temple with the grip-end.

Action M

- Step forward with the left foot and defend P's hit with your shield.

Phase 13 - PIERCE ABDOMEN

Action P

- Remaining with the left foot in front, swing the spearhead upwards on your left side and pierce M's lower abdomen.

Action M

- Remaining with the left foot in front, push down the spearhead with both weapons.

Phase 14 - TROT AND PIERCE RIGHT TEMPLE

Action P

- Trot forward with the left foot leading and pierce M's right temple with the spearhead.

Action M

- Trot backwards with the right foot in the rear and deflect P's attack with your sword.

Phase 15 - STEP RIGHT AND HIT ANKLE

Action P

- Step forward with the right foot and hit M's right inner ankle by swinging the grip-end of the spear diagonally down.

Action M

- Step backwards with the left foot and defend P's hit at the right ankle with your sword.

Phase 16 - PRESS DOWN SWORD

Action P

- Step backwards with the left foot and turning your body a little to the left, crouch and press down the sword to the floor, with the grip-end of your spear and thus defend M's cut at your left ribs.

Action M

- Stepping forward with the right foot, cut P's left ribs with the sword.

Phase 17 - DEFEND ANKLE AND SWIRL

Action P

- Step backwards with the right foot and defend M's cut at your left inner ankle with the spearhead.
- Then scoop up and swirl the sword towards the left and press it on the floor.

Action M

- Step forward with the left foot and cut at P's left inner ankle with your sword.
- Then your sword gets scooped and swirled.

Phase 18 - STEP RIGHT AND HIT ABDOMEN

Action P

- Step forward with the left foot and hit at M's lower abdomen, with the grip-end of your spear with an upward swing.

Action M

- Retreat the left foot and defend P's hit on your abdomen, by pressing down the spear with your weapons.

Phase 19 - STEP LEFT AND HIT ABDOMEN

Action P

- Step forward with the left foot and hit at M's lower abdomen with an upward swing of the spearhead.

Action M

- Retreat the right foot and defend P's hit on abdomen, by pressing down the spear with both your weapons.

Phase 20 - HIT HEAD WITH RIGHT IN FRONT

Action P

- Remaining with the right foot in front, hit at M's head, with the grip-end of the spear.

Action M

- Remaining with the right foot in front, defend P's hit at your head by lifting both your weapons overhead.

Phase 21 - PIERCE FOOT WITH LEFT FOOT LEADING

Action P

- With the left foot in front, pierce M's left foot, with the spearhead.

Action M

- With the left foot leading, swing aside P's attack with your sword.

Phase 22 - TURN JUMPING, DEFEND ANKLE

Action P

- Lift the left foot to the level of your right inner knee while rotating the spearhead once in an anti-clockwise direction on the left side close to your body.
- Pointing the spearhead towards M's chest, step forward, diagonally a little towards your right side, with the left foot. Then take off on your left foot and land forward on your right foot.
- Simultaneously, swival by your left to the opposite direction, place your left foot in the rear with a long step, and defend M's cut aimed at your right inner ankle with the grip-end swung down.

Action M

- Retreat with your right foot and lift the left foot to the level of your right inner knee.
- Move down the left foot and keep it diagonally a little towards your right side, a little ahead. Then take off on it and land forward on your right foot.
- Simultaneously, swival by your left to the opposite direction, place your left foot in the rear with a long step. While swivaling, swing the sword overhead in a clockwise direction, and after landing and facing P swing down a cut at P's inner right ankle.

Phase 23 - RETREAT TROT AND DEFEND ANKLE

Action P

- Step backwards with the left and then with the right foot, pointing the spearhead at M's chest.
- Trot backwards with the right foot in the rear.
- Then step back with the left foot and defend M's cut aimed at your right inner ankle, with the grip-end of your spear.

Action M

- Step forward with the right and then with the left foot.
- Trot forward with the left foot in front.
- Step forward with your right foot and aim a cut, with the sword, at P's inner right ankle.

Phase 24 - RETREAT RIGHT AND HIT TEMPLE

Action P

- Step backwards with the right foot and hit at M's right temple with the spearhead.

Action M

- Step forward with the left foot and defend P's hit at your right temple with the sword.

Phase 25 - RECEIVE CUT ON HEAD

Action P

- Remaining with the left foot in front, defend M's cut on your head, receiving the cut in the middle of the spear between the grips by lifting it overhead, slightly to the front.
- While defending, the spearhead remains pointing to your left side.

Action M

- Remaining with the left foot in front, execute a vertical cut at P's head with your sword.

Phase 26 - RETREAT RIGHT AND PRESS DOWN SWORD

Action P

- Step backwards with the right foot.
- Simultaneously, lift the grip-end of your spear and move it from the left to your right in an arc-wise manner and press down M's sword with the grip-end itself on your right side in a 'crouch' posture.

Action M

- Step forward with the left and aim a thrust with the tip of the sword at P's right ribs.

Phase 27 - STEP LEFT AND HIT ANKLE

Action P

- Stepping forward with the left foot, aim a hit at M's left inner ankle with the spearhead.

Action M

- Stepping backwards with the right foot, defend P's attack with your sword.

Phase 28 - TURN JUMPING, PRESS DOWN SWORD

Action P

- Repeat Phase 22 but instead of defending the ankle, press down M's cut aimed at your left ribs with the grip-end of the spear as in Phase 16.

Action M

- Repeat Phase 22, but instead of aiming at P's ankle, aim a cut at P's left ribs as in Phase 16.

Phase 29 - TROT AND PIERCE CHEST

Action P

- From the 'crouch' posture, stand up and step forward with the left foot.
- While stepping forward, brandish a hit at M's right ribs with the grip-end of your spear, moving it from the left to right.
- Without breaking the flow of the spear, move the grip-end further till the spearhead points at M's chest.
- Trot forward with the left foot in front, and pierce M's chest with the spearhead by stretching your arms forward.

Action M

- Stand up and step backwards with the right foot and thus avert P's hit on your right ribs.
- Then trot backwards with the right foot in the rear and defend P's attack aimed at your chest by deflecting the spear upwards by lifting your weapons crossed overhead.

ORAL COMMANDS

Salutation

Rotate Spearhead, Step Right and Hit Head (Phase 1), Step Left and Pierce Abdomen (Phase 2), Trot Back and Crouch (Phase 3)

First Series

A. Step Right and Hit Head (4).

B. Retreat Right and Defend Ankle (5), Hit Head (6), Retreat Left and Hit Head (7), Step Back and Pierce Foot (8), Hit Temple (9).

C. Step Right and Left and Pierce (10), Retreat Left and Defend Ankle (11), Retreat Right and Hit Temple (12), Pierce Abdomen (13), Hit Head (6), Retreat Left and Hit Head (7), Step Back and Pierce Foot (8), Hit Temple (9), Trot Back and Crouch (3).

Second Series

A. Trot and Pierce Right Temple (14), Step Right and Hit Ankle (15).

B. Retreat Right and Hit Temple (12), Pierce Abdomen (13), Hit Head (6), Retreat Left and Hit Head (7), Step Back and Pierce Foot (8), Hit Temple (9).

C. *Repeat C of the First Series.*

Third Series

A. *Repeat A of the Second Series.*

B. *Repeat B of the Second Series.*

C. Step Right and Left and Pierce (10), Retreat Left and Defend Ankle (11), Retreat Right and Hit Temple (12), Pierce Abdomen (13), Hit Head (6), Retreat Left and Hit Head (7), Step Back and Pierce Foot (8), Hit Temple (9).

D. Step Right and Left and Pierce (10), Press Down Sword (16), Defend Ankle and Swirl (17), Hit Temple (9).

E. Step Right and Hit Abdomen (18), Step Left and Hit Abdomen (19), Step Right and Hit Abdomen (18), Hit Head with Right in Front (20), Pierce Foot with Left Foot Leading (21), Hit Temple (9), Turn Jumping, Defend Ankle (22), Retreat Right and Hit Temple (12), Pierce Foot with Left Foot Leading (21), Hit Temple (9).

F. *Repeat Phases under D.*

G. *Repeat Phases under E.*

H. *Repeat C of First Series.*

Fourth Series

A. Trot and Pierce RightTemple (14).

B. Retreat, Trot and Defend Ankle (23), Retreat Right and Hit Temple (24), Receive Cut on Head (25), Press Down Sword (16), Retreat Right and Press Down Sword (26), Retreat Left and Defend Ankle (11), Hit Head with Right in Front (20), Step Left and Hit Ankle (27), Hit Temple (9).

C. Step Right and Left and Pierce (10), Press Down Sword (16), Defend Ankle and Swirl (17), Hit Temple (9).

D. Step Right and Hit Abdomen (18), Step Left and Hit Abdomen (19), Step Right and Hit Abdomen (18), Hit Head with Right in Front (20), Step Left and Hit Ankle (27), Hit Temple (9), Turn Jumping, Press Down Sword (28), Defend Ankle and Swirl (17), Hit Temple (9).

E. *Repeat Phases under C.*

F. *Repeat Phases under D.*

G. *Repeat C of First Series.*

Fifth Series

A. Trot and Pierce Right Temple (14).

B. Press Down Sword (16), Trot and Pierce Chest (29), Step Right and Hit Head (4), Retreat Right and Hit Temple (24), Pierce Foot with Left Foot Leading (21), Hit Temple (9).

C. Step Right and Left and Pierce (10), Press Down Sword (16), Defend Ankle and Swirl (17), Hit Temple (9).

D. *Repeat Phases under D of Fourth Series.*

E. *Repeat Phases under C of Fourth Series.*

F. *Repeat Phases under D of Fourth Series.*

G. *Repeat C of First Series.*

TECHNIQUES OF BARE-HANDED DEFENCE AND ATTACK

(*Verumkai*)

You have developed a strong and agile physique by practising the series in *maippayattu* and have achieved skill in wielding weapons by practising the series in *kolethaari* and *angathaari*. You are now ready for *verumkaippayattu*, the last series in *payattu*.

The word *verum-kai* in Malayalam means bare hand. As is obvious, the techniques in *verumkai* prepare one to defend an opponent's armed or unarmed onslaught and attack him with bare hands and legs.

Many of the postures, already learnt and perfected in *maippayattu*, find practical application in the *verumkai* techniques of *payattu*. Similarly the forward, backward and sideways movements, trots, leaps, kicks and jabs learnt initially come in handy in *verumkai*.

Verumkaippayattu enables one to either keep an opponent at bay or to disable him.

While defending and attacking, one must assume a well-balanced, strong and stable posture. From this posture, the arms, hands, legs, feet and trunk should move quickly and forcefully in a controlled explosion of energy. One must apply the techniques with the greatest speed possible so as to achieve the best and most effective results.

Various kinds of blocks, cuts, thrusts, kicks, trots, leaps, throws and sideways swinging movements are used. The forearm, outer edge of the palm and foot, fist, fingers, elbows and knees are used to defend and attack. Several techniques to lock and break an opponent's arms, fingers, neck, ribs and backbone are employed. There are techniques by which an opponent is lifted off his feet and thrown up or dashed to the floor.

During this advanced and final stage of *payattu* training, the guru teaches a select few of his most disciplined students about *marmas* or the vital points of the body. By applying force or inflicting cuts on *marmas* one could cause pain to an opponent, cause temporary or permanent injury, maim or even cause death. It is in *verumkai* more than in any other group in *payattu*, that one gets direct chances of using the *marma* techniques.

In their ancient texts, Shushrutha and Vakbhata in Sanskrit, and Agasthya in Tamil, have explained *marmas* and identified one hundred and eight vital points of the human body. *Kalarippayattu* preceptors have classified sixty-four such spots as *kulaabhyaasa marmangal.* It is not within the scope of this book to give details on this subject or on the *marma* techniques.

Physical strength, stamina, quick reflexes of the body and mind and ability to concentrate on the onslaught are vital in facing and vanquishing an opponent, especially when one is bare-handed.

In olden days, those training in *payattu* used to practise certain exercises especially meant for developing physical strength. One of them was a form of weight-lifting. The trainees lifted round metalic boulders from the ground and threw them overhead, and repeated this many times. In the present day context, the trainees could instead exercise with dumb-bells and train with weights.

Explained in this section are just a few of the numerous *verumkai* techniques. The selection is made based on the ease of application and effectiveness of the techniques.

The movements of the hands, legs and body should be well coordinated and synchronized. A student may start slowly, yet systematically practise all the techniques, and then gradually increase the speed and force. Depending on the actual situation, one may adapt the techniques while defending and attacking.

While learning and practising the *verumkai* techniques, take care not to hurt your sparring partner.

BARE-HANDED DEFENCE TECHNIQUES

DODGE (Methods of Dodging)

1. STEP AND CROUCH

- When an opponent hits at your left temple, dodge it by stepping forward with the right foot, diagonally to the left side. Simultaneously, duck with a 'crouch'.
- Simultaneously, rise and turn your body towards the right to be behind the opponent.

2. SIT SIDEWAYS

- When an opponent hits at your left temple, dodge it by moving the left foot further towards the left. Here the body-weight should be shifted on to your left foot (as in Phase 71 of *Otta Payattu*, do the 'Sit Sideways' part), while the right leg is held stretched straight.

3. SIT BACKWARDS

- When an opponent hits at your temple, dodge it by taking a long right or left step backwards (as in Phase 41 or 42 of *Maippayattu*, do only the 'Sit' part). Here the body-weight should be shifted on to your rear leg, the knee held bent. The other leg is held stretched straight in front.

4. STEP DIAGONALLY

- When an opponent thrusts his clenched fist or a dagger at your abdomen, dodge it by stepping forward with a long right step towards the right side of the opponent.

5. TROT BACKWARDS

- When an opponent moves forward with multiple steps to attack you, dodge him by trotting backwards (as in Phase 12 of *Muchaan Payattu*, do M's action), either by crouching or holding your body upright

STRIDE (Methods of striding)

1. STRIDE, DEFENDING CHEST

- Trot forward towards the opponent with your body leaning slightly forward or in a crouched posture, with the left foot in front. The forearms are crossed in front, protecting your chest.
  (This helps you to be in readiness to effectively defend the opponent's attacks and also to deliver attacks at the opponent in front.)

2. STRIDE, DEFENDING HEAD

- While facing the opponent in front, step forward in a crouched posture with your left foot, your body leaning slightly forward. While striding forward, your left forearm is held overhead slightly to the front ready to defend your head; the right arm is kept free to attack or defend.

BLOCK (Methods of Blocking)

A. SINGLE-HANDED BLOCKS

1. When an opponent in front aims a hit at your left temple, step forward with your left foot, raise the left hand overhead, slightly to the front, and thus block the attack with your left palm facing outward, just below the opponent's wrist.

2. When an opponent in front aims a thrust with his fist or stabs at the right side of your abdomen, step forward with your right foot, diagonally to your left. Simultaneously, push away the opponent's thrust before it reaches the target by swinging your right arm in an anti-clockwise manner in front of your body.

3. When an opponent in front aims a hit at your left temple, step forward with the left, diagonally to your left. Swing your left hand from left to right to move along with the opponent's hit (arm) in the same direction and thus jab-off the attack downward.

B. DOUBLE-HANDED BLOCKS

1. When an opponent in front aims a hit at your left temple, step forward with the right foot and turn your body to the left. Raise both your arms in front, and thus block the attack with your palms just below the opponent's wrist or in the middle of the forearm.

2. When an opponent in front delivers a thrust aimed at the right side of your abdomen, step forward with your left, diagonally slightly to the left. Simultaneously, turn your body fully to the right side. Then with your arms bent, block at the opponent's elbow with your palms.

3. When an opponent in front aims a hit at the left side of your body, step forward with the right towards the left side of the opponent. Simultaneously, turn your body fully to the left side. Then thrust your arms forward and thus block the opponent's right forearm with your palms.

4. When an opponent in front aims a hit at your left temple, step forward with the right and turn your body to the left. Simultaneously, with your palms held together and the fingers intertwined, hammer down the opponent's right hand with your outer left fist.

5. When an opponent in front aims a hit at your left temple, step forward with the right foot. Simultaneously, with your right forearm held horizontally in front, block the hit. While blocking the attack, support your right arm by holding the palms together.

6. When an opponent in front stabs or hits at the left side of your abdomen, step forward with the right foot, turn your body completely to the left. In the crouched posture, block the stab or hit with your forearms held vertically in front. The point of contact is just below the opponent's wrist.

7. When an opponent aims a kick with his right leg at your left abdomen, block it with your forearms as explained in B6.

C. FORKED-HANDED BLOCKS

1. When an opponent in front aims a hit on your head, step forward with the left or right foot. Simultaneously, raise your arms crossed overhead, slightly to the front. Receive the hit midway at the fork of your crossed arms

2. When an opponent in front aims a thrust at your abdomen, with your left foot in front, push down the thrust with the fork of your crossed forearms. Here your right forearm remains over the left.

D. HIP BLOCK

When an opponent aims a kick horizontally with his right foot at your left flank, step forward with your left, diagonally slightly towards the left. Then advance a step with the right, and simultaneously turn by the left to the opposite direction to be very close to the opponent. Block at the right inner thigh of the opponent with your right hip.

E. LEG BLOCK

When an opponent in front aims a hit at the left side of your body, with your left foot in front, swing 'Inward Right' as in Phase 26 of *Maippayattu* at an appropriate level and thus defend the hit with your right instep at the forearm of the opponent.

DEFENCE AND COUNTER-ATTACKS

METHODS OF DEFENCE AND COUNTER ATTACKS

1. After blocking the opponent's hit (as in Block AI), step forward with the right and jab your right elbow forward and attack the opponent's chest in the middle.

2. When an opponent aims a hit at your left temple, step forward with the left, block the hit with your left hand (as in Block AI) at the wrist of the opponent. Simultaneously, deliver a hit at the opponent's eyes with your right palm, fingers pointing towards the left. Kick at the opponent's groin with the outer edge of your right foot. Both these attacks should be done together.

3. After blocking the opponent's attack (as in Block AI), step forward with your right foot and hit at the nose and forehead of the opponent, with your right palm, fingers turned upwards.

4. After blocking the opponent's attack (as in Block BI), lift your right elbow to thrust at the opponent's ribs just below the right armpit.

5. After blocking the opponent's attack (as in Block Bl), cut at the right side of the opponent's neck below the ear with the outer edge of your right hand, palm turned downward.

6. After blocking the opponent's attack (as in Block B2), lift your left elbow and thrust with it at the opponent's right ribs.

7. After blocking the opponent's attack (as in Block B2), lift your left palm, hit at the opponent's eyes, the tip of your fingers pointing towards the left of the opponent's face.

8. After blocking the opponent's thrust (as in Block B3), thrust your right elbow forward at the opponent's chest. Here your target of attack is the opponent's chest, below his right nipple.

9. After blocking the opponent's thrust (as in Block B3), cut at the opponent's neck on the right side, with the outer edge of your right hand.

10. After blocking the opponent's hit (as in Block B4), swing your clenched arms to hammer a hit at the opponent's right temple. Here the hit is delivered with the right outer fist.

11. After blocking the opponent's attack (as in Block B5), with your clenched left fist, deliver a punch at the right ribs near his right nipple. While doing this, your right hand should be held blocking the opponent's hit.

12. After blocking the opponent's attack (as in Block B6), thrust your right elbow below the opponent's right nipple.

13. After blocking the opponent's hit (as in Block B6), snap at his scrotum, with the knuckle of your clenched right first.

14. After blocking the opponent's hit (as in Block Cl), jerk your right knee upwards to attack his groin.

15. After blocking the opponent's attack (as in Block C2), lift your right hand and hit at his right temple with the knuckle of your clenched right fist.

COUNTER TRICKS

METHODS OF COUNTER TRICKS

1. • When an opponent standing in front, tries to strangle you with both hands, place your right palm firmly over the opponent's right wrist, your right forearm below his left forearm.
   • Then, with a rapid upward jerk of your right elbow, push up the opponent's left hand. Continuing, bend your body towards the left, stepping your right foot towards the left side.

2. When an opponent standing in front grabs around your waist, place your left palm firmly at the back of his head, and press his nose upwards from below with the base of your right palm. Then, step forward with your right and push the opponent backwards.

3. When an opponent standing in front grips your right wrist with his right hand, place your left palm firmly over his grip. Then wind your right hand clockwise around his hand, hold it firmly over his wrist. Stepping back with your right foot, pull his arm towards the right while pressing it downwards.

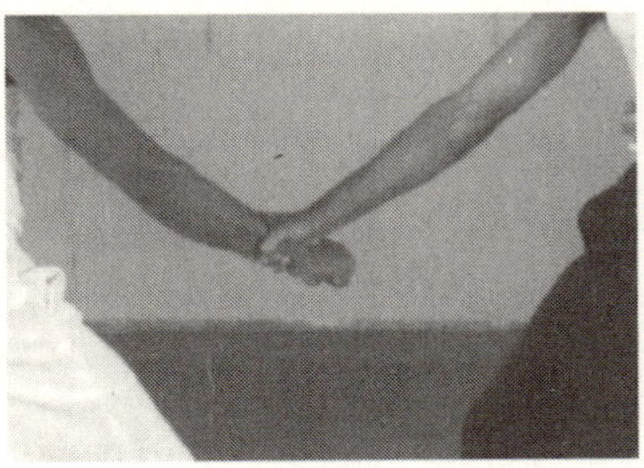
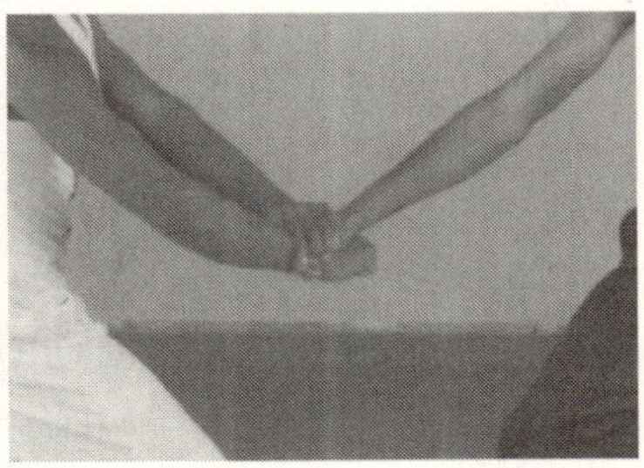
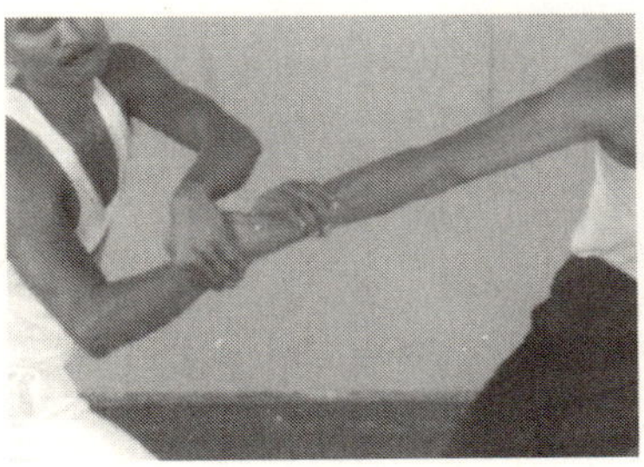

4. When an opponent strangles you from behind, hold his little fingers and tear them apart with a sharp motion.

5. When an opponent standing in front catches your collar with his left hand, place your left hand firmly over his hand. Then hit at his eyes with the flat of your right hand, fingers turned to the left.

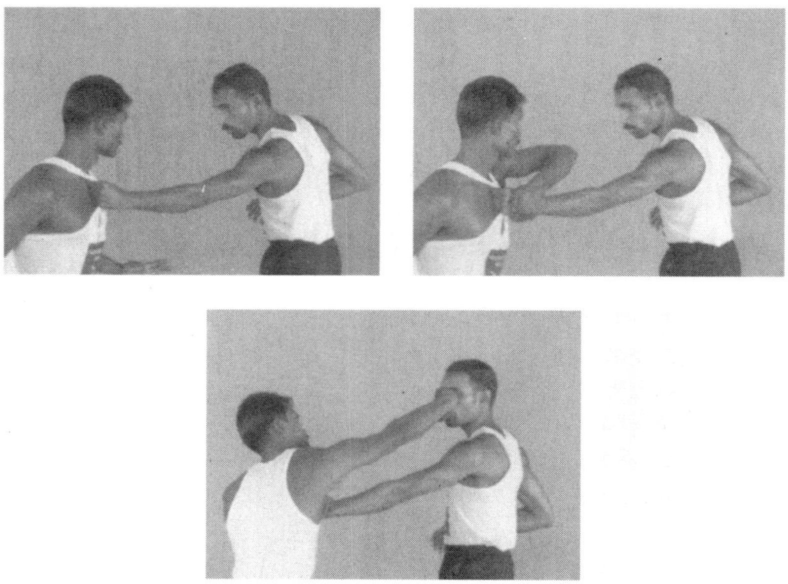

6. When an opponent tries to break your right hand by interlocking his right hand fingers with yours, straighten the fingers of your right hand, place the index finger of your left hand below and at the base of your fingers. Then with a sharp motion, bend the opponent's fingers backwards and break them.

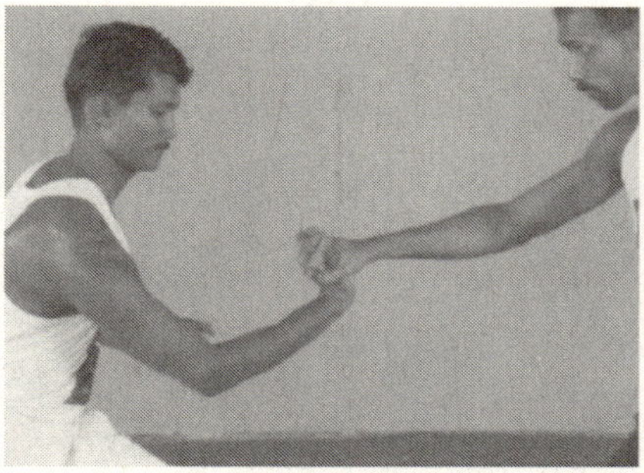

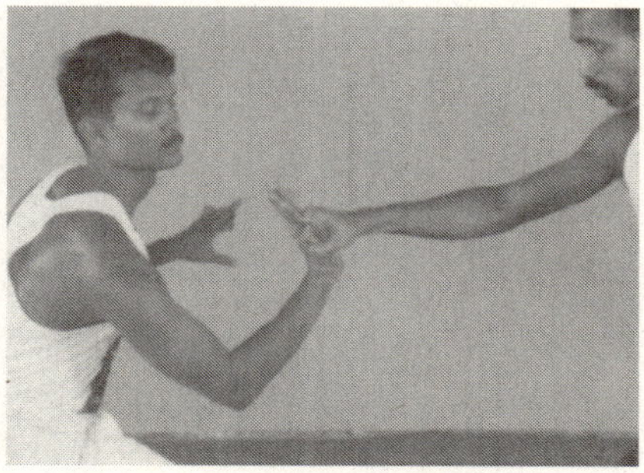

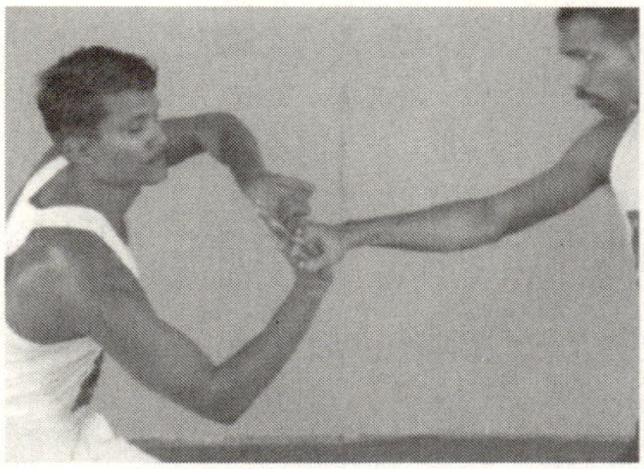

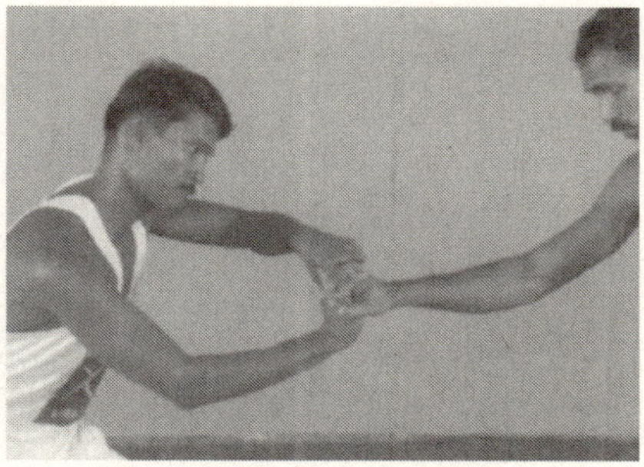

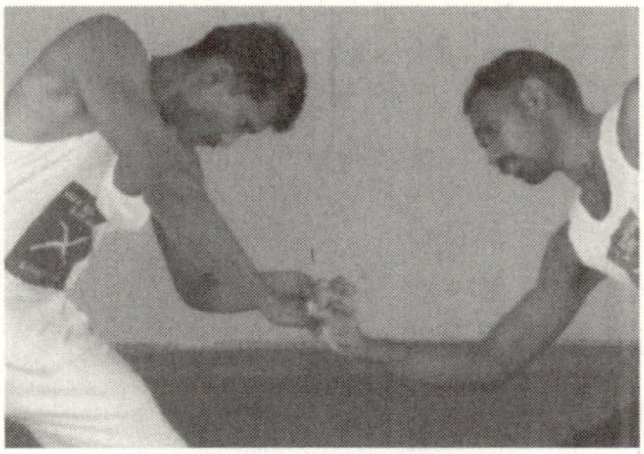

7. When an opponent standing on your right side tries to strangle you with both his hands, lift your right arm through the opponent's hold. Then move your right arm backwards, lock the opponent's left arm by holding it around. In a simultaneous action, bend your body backwards, lift your right arm and thus break the opponent's locked left elbow.

8. When an opponent grabs you around your waist from behind, bend your body forward a little, stamp on any one of the opponent's feet, which ever is in front, with your right or left heel as is convenient.

THROWS, SMASH, THRUST AND BREAKS

Methods of Disabling an Opponent

THROWS

1. After blocking the opponent's hit aimed at your left temple (as in Block AI), step forward with your right foot and assume a crouch posture. Then pull the opponent's right hand with your left hand further towards the left over your shoulders. Push your right hand through the legs of the opponent and hold his right thigh. Hold the opponent's right arm behind the back of your neck. With the help of the right shoulder, lift the opponent and throw him over.

2. After blocking the opponent's hit aimed at your left temple (as in Block AI), step forward diagonally with your right foot towards his right side. Keep your right leg behind the opponent's right leg, crossing it at the knee joint behind. Hold the opponent's neck with your right hand, and then throw him backwards on to the floor.

3. After blocking the opponent's hit aimed at your left temple (as in Block AI), step forward diagonally with your right foot towards the opponent's right side. Holding the arrested hand at the wrist with your left hand, keep your right elbow joint under the opponent's right elbow. Push at the opponent's chin with your right hand and throw him backwards on to the floor.

4. After defending the opponent's hit (as in Block AI), continue the anti-clockwise movement of your arm to bring the opponent's arm down in front of the right thigh. Step forward diagonally with your right foot towards the back of the opponent, hold his neck with the right arm and throw him backwards on to the floor.

SMASH

Step forward with your right and arrest the opponent's right-handed hit aimed at your left temple by lifting your right hand. The point of contact is at the opponent's wrist. Receive the hit with your right palm, the fingers pointing to the left. Then stretch your left arm in front of the opponent's arrested right arm through to the back of his neck. Pull his body downward. In a simultaneous action, lift your left knee to smash the opponent's face.

THRUST

Step forward with your right and arrest the opponent's right-handed hit aimed at your left temple by lifting your right hand. The point of contact is at the opponent's wrist. Receive the hit with your right palm, the fingers pointing to the left.

Then step forward with your left foot towards the opponent's left side.

Insert your left arm through the left armpit of the opponent.

Simultaneously, pull the opponent's arrested arm over his head to his back.

Hold the opponent's right palm behind his back with your left hand.

Free your right hand.

Bend the opponent backwards by pulling the arrested hand, and land him on to your left bent knee. And with your right elbow, thrust at the opponent's chest.

BREAKS

1. After arresting the opponent's thrust (as in Block A2), continue the anti-clockwise motion of your arm and lift the opponent's arrested arm to his shoulder level.
   Then moving towards the back of the opponent, hold his arm and neck with your right hand, your palm resting on the opponent's left shoulder.
   Bend him backwards, while pushing at the opponent's backbone with your left hand.

2. After arresting the opponent's attack (as in Block BI), step forward with your right diagonally to the left, to the opponent's right side. Turn by the left to the opposite direction. Here your opponent is behind you. Bring the opponent's right arm on to your left shoulder, and pull it downwards, at the same time pushing the opponent's elbow joint upwards with your shoulder to break the opponent's arm.

3. After arresting the opponent's hit aimed at the right side of your abdomen (as in Block B2), hold his right wrist with your right hand.
   Simultaneously, push at the opponent's right elbow, with your left palm, fingers pointed upwards.
   Pull the opponent's right wrist so as to break his elbow-joint.

4. After arresting the opponent's stab or hit (as in Block B6), hold his arrested wrist with your left hand, place your right forearm below the opponent's right elbow joint.
   Hold your left wrist with your right hand and bend the opponent's right hand backwards.
   Bend it further and break it.

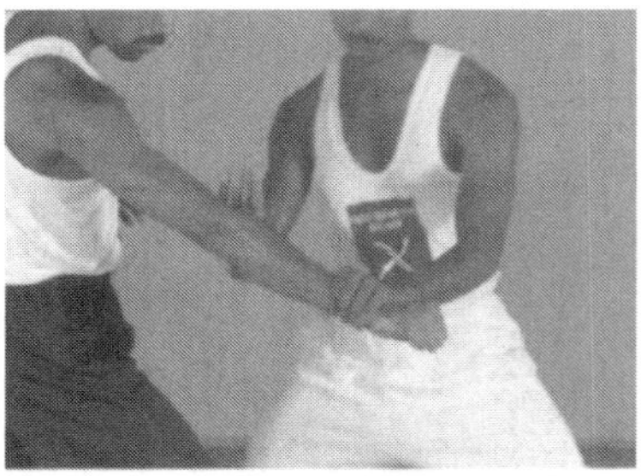

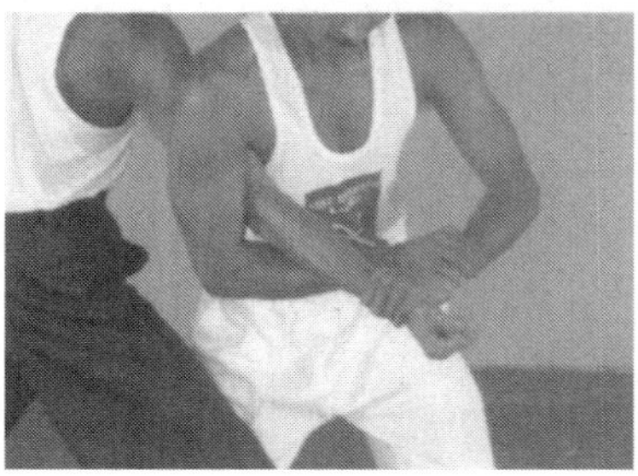

5. After arresting the opponent's stab or hit aimed at your left temple, hold his arrested wrist with your left hand, bring your right hand below the opponent's right wrist, hold his thumb and lobe from below.
Step back with your left foot and twist the opponent's hand backward till it breaks.

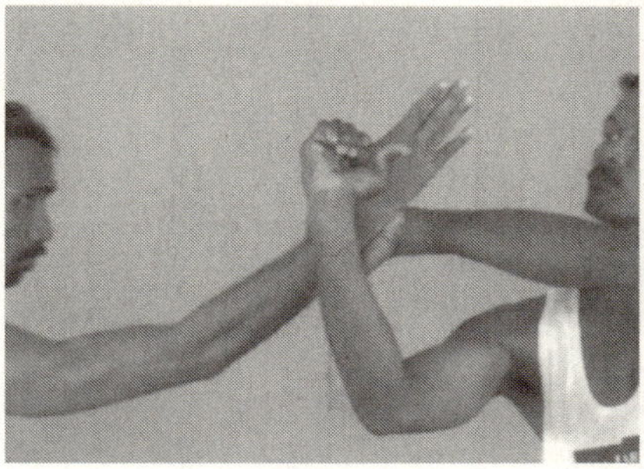

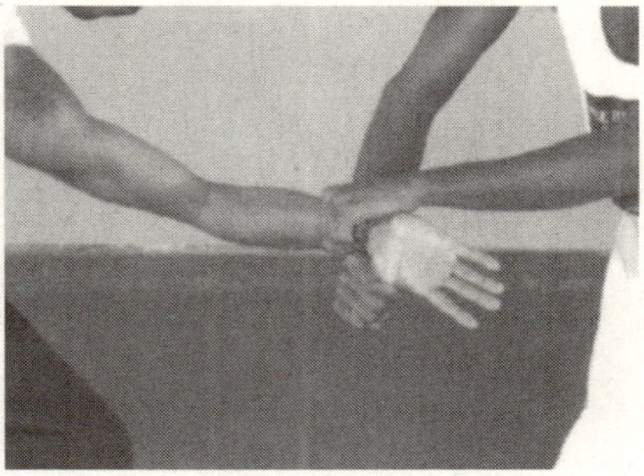

6. Step forward with your right and arrest the opponent's right-handed hit aimed at your left temple.
   This is done by lifting your right hand in front, receiving the hit with your palm, fingers pointing to the left.
   Then hold the opponent's wrist.
   Thereafter, step forward with your left towards the right side of the opponent.
   Push at the opponent's right elbow joint upwards and twist his right arm backwards, your right hand still gripping the opponent's wrist.
   The twisted arm of the opponent is thus brought behind his back.
   Push the hand upwards to break the opponent's shoulder joint.
   Simultaneously hold the opponent's neck with your left forearm and press his adam's apple.

GLOSSARY

angathaari (*anga-thaa-ri*): The group of exercises in *payattu* where shield and sharp weapons such as swords, spears, urumi and daggers are used.

ankam (*ankam*): A duel between two hired mercenaries on behalf of two rival groups or families.

anpatheerati kalari (*an-pa-thee-rati, ka-la-ri*): A *kalari* admeasuring fifty two feet in length and twenty six feet in breadth.

arappukkai (*ara-ppu-kai*): A *payattu* style which is the most popular and superior to other *payattu* styles. The exercises explained in this book are from the *arappukkai* style of *payattu.*

asthadikapalas (*ashta-dik-paalaas*): According to Hindu belief, the Lords protecting or guarding the eight corners of the universe.

asura (*asu-ra*): Demon

ayurveda (*aa-yoor-veda*): An ancient form of medical science, evolved, developed and practiced to this day in India.

bana (*baa-na*): A technique akin to *pandeeran veeshal* of *kalarippayattu*, which is popular in Central India.

Bhadra (*bhadra*): The Hindu godess who is worshipped as the one presiding deity of war.

Bhargava (*bhaar-ga-va*): Another name of Parashurama.

chekon (*che-kon*): A soldier who was hired to fight an *ankam.*

Chengannuradi (*chen-gannoor-aad*): A character described in *thekkan pattukal* who was an expert in martial arts.

Cheras (*che-raas*): *A* royal family of Tamil Nadu which ruled over Kerala during 8th through to 11th century.

cherukalari (*cheru-ka-la-ri*): A small *kalari*

cheruvati (*che-ru-va-ti*): Another name for short-staff (see *muchaan)*

Chirakkal (*chi-ra-kkal*): A village, about five kilometres north of Kannur in North Malabar. Sreedharan Nair, the author of this book, hailed from this village.

churika (*chu-ri-ka*): A special kind of sword.

dakshina (*dak-shi-na*): The Malayalam word for cash or other offerings given to a guru, teacher or priest.

deva (*de-va*): God

dhanur veda (*dha-nur, ve-da*): The ancient treatise on weapons and weapons training, originally written in Sanskrit.

dronamballi (*dro-nam-balli*): A style of *payattu*, now extinct.

Embrandiri (*em-braan-di-ri*): Brahmins from Tulu Nadu settled in North Malabar for generations.

garadi (*ga-ra-di*): A martial art form peculiar to Tulu Nadu in Karnataka State, now practically extinct.

gotra (*go-thra*): Clan

guruthara (*guru-tha-ra*): The seat dedicated to the preceptors of *kalarippayattu*, normally between the western main pillar and the *poothara.*

Iravikutty Pillai (*iravi-ku-tty, pilla*): The name of an expert in *kalarippayattu* who lived in the southern part of Kerala.

Itanatan (*ita-naa-tan*): The name of an expert in *kalarippayattu* who lived in the southern part of Kerala.

kacha (*ka-cha*): A unique kind of loin-cloth which is a long cotton cloth used as a supporter by those practicing in a *kalari*. This cloth is worn around one's waist in a particular fashion.

kathakali (*ka-tha-ka-li*): A highly stylised dance-drama peculiar to Kerala where the dancers wear bright coloured head-gear and dress to appear larger than life characters representing Hindu gods, demons and mythological demi-gods.

kalari (*ka-la-ri*): A specially constructed gymnasium where *kalarippayattu* is taught.

kalarippayattu (*ka-la-ri, pa-ya-ttu*): *Kalari* plus *payattu*. The ancient martial art peculiar to Kerala, taught in a specially constructed gymnasium called *kalari*.

Kari Gurukkal (*kaa-ri, gu-ru-kkal*): A *pulaya* (Hindu low-caste untouchable) boy who became an expert in *kalarippayattu* and eventually became a *gurukkal* (or guru). He learnt black magic and could change himself into animals. The legend has it that he transformed himself as a leopard and could not come back to his original human form. He was deified and is enacted as *theyyam* and worshipped to this day.

kattara, kattaram (*ka-ttaa-ra, ka-ttaa-ram*): A dagger.

kavu (*kaa-vu*): A tribal temple.

kettukaari (*kettu-kaa-ri*): A five-foot long cane or bamboo staff used in *payattu*.

khedam (*khe-dam*): A Tamil word for shield.

Kolathiri (*kola-thi-ri*): A royal family in North Malabar. Chirakkal is the seat of this royal family. Sreedharan Nair's father, Rama Varma Valiya Raja was the head of the Kolathiri Royal Family for almost thirty five years upto 1952.

kolkali (*kol-ka-li*): A group dance, where male dancers, dance around in a circle, to the accompaniment of songs, tapping small sticks held in both hands in a rhythmic fashion.

kolethaari (*kol-thaa-ri*): Exercises done with wooden weapons.

Konkan (*kon-kan*): Konkan region is the land that stretches in the north of Tulu Nadu, along the western ghats.

kootiyattam (*kooti-yaa-ttam*): The form of Sanskrit drama which exists in Kerala.

Kautilya (*kau-ti-llya*): A Sanskrit scholar of yore who wrote, Arthashastra.

kovilakam (*ko-vi-la-kam*): A house where the members of the Royal Family in Kerala reside.

kurichiya (*ku-ri-chi-ya*): A tribal clan who live in the hilly region of Malabar. They are expert hunters and were believed to be brave and ferocious.

kurumkalari (*kurum-ka-la-ri*): Small *kalari*.

langotti (*lan-go-tti*): Loin-cloth stitched into shape, used as a supporter by those practicing in a *kalari*.

maippayattu (*mai-pa-ya-ttu*): Mai plus *payattu*. *Mai* in Malayalam means body. Hence, a series of body exercises or conditionals.

maiyirakku (*mai-ira-kku*): Another name of *maippayattu*.

Malayalam (*ma-la-yaa-lam*): The language of Kerala. The original oral command (or *vaaithaari*) of *payattu* is in Malayalam.

Mannappan (*ma-nna-ppan*): A *Thiyya* (a Hindu low caste) youth who was an expert in *payattu*. He is believed to have been slain in a fight in the hilly terrain of Kotaku in Karnataka State. Later deified and continues to be worshipped by the people of Malabar as Kativannoor Veeran.

marma darpanam (*mar-ma, dar-pa-nam*): *Marma* is the Malayalam word for vital point of the human body. *Darpanam* means mirror. Hence, *Marma Darpanam* mean 'the mirror of marma'. Chirakkal T.Sreedharan Nair authored a book on the vital points of the human body and entitled it as 'Marma Darpanam'.

mara pitichu kuntha payattu (*ma-ra, pi-ti-chu, kun-tha, pa-ya-ttu*): A unique method of fighting in *payattu* where one wields a spear, while the other wields a sword and shield.

marmam (*mar-mam*): Vital point of the body.

muchaan (*mu-chaan*): A wooden weapon, about two feet long, tapering from the grip-end to the hit-end.

muppatheerati kalari (*muppa-thee-ra-ti, ka-la-ri*): A *kalari* which is thirty two feet long and sixteen feet wide.

mutiyettu (*mu-ti-ye-ttu*): A traditional folk-art form popular in South Kerala.

nayaattu (*naa-yaa-ttu*): The Malayalam word for hunting.

Nair, Nayar (*naa-yar*): A Hindu high caste, of Kerala. Nairs were traditionally warriors.

nalppatheerati kalari (*naal-ppa-thee-ra-ti, ka-la-ri*): A *kalari* admeasuring forty two feet in length and twenty one feet in breadth.

Namboothiris (*nam-boo-thi-ris*): The Aryan descendents of Kerala Brahmins.

netumkalari (*ne-tum-ka-la-ri*): A large *kalari.*

nritham (*nri-tham*): A peculiar dance-form performed in many temples of Malabar where the *Embrandiri* (Brahmin) priests carrying the god's decorated idol on their head and perform the dance.

otimurissery (*oti-muri-ssery*): A style of *payattu* where bone-setting techniques are also taught. Was popular in Central Kerala.

otta (*o-tta*): A wooden weapon with double curves, shaped as a horn.

pandeeran (*pan-dee-ran*): The five-foot long cane or bamboo staff used in *payattu* by individual atheletes to wield at imaginary opponents.

pakarchakkal (*pa-kar-cha-kkaal*): An advanced series of *maippayattu.*

pantheerati kalari (*pan-thee-ra-ti, ka-la-ri*): A *kalari* which is twelve-feet long and six feet wide.

Parashurama (*pa-ra-shu-raa-ma*): A warrior-sage, believed to be an immortal, according to Hindu mythology. Believed to have created Kerala from the Arabian sea. Believed also to be the originator or *kalarippayattu.*

parichamuttukali (*pa-ri-cha-muttu-ka-li*): A ritualistic folk-art form popular in South Kerala where the performers wield a sword and shield.

patayani (*pa-ta-ya-ni*): A ritualistic group-dance, popular in South Kerala. Here the performers wear large headgears and represent dieties, demons and animals, and go around dancing to the rhythm of drumbeats and songs.

pathinetteerati kalari (*pa-thi-nettee-ra-ti, ka-la-ri*): A *kalari* which is twenty feet long and ten feet wide.

payattu (*pa-ya-ttu*): An ancient martial art peculiar to Kerala.

Payyamballi Chandu (*payyam-ba-lli, chan-du*): A great expert in *payattu.* There are tales of his valour in the Ballads of North Malabar.

Pazhashi (*pazha-shi*): A village in North Malabar which was ruled by a royal family there, hence Pazhashi Raja (the Raja of Pazhashi).

Perumals (*peru-maals*): Another name for Cheras.

pillathangi (*pilla-thaan-gi*): A *payattu* style popular in the southern parts of Malabar.

poithu (*poi-thu*): A duel betwen two individuals to settle their personal quarrels.

poorakali (*poo-ra-kka-li*): A folk-art form of North Malabar. In it there are two distinct forms, one transcends to the level of intellectual extravaganza, the other is a group dance by male dancers.

poothara (*poo-tha-ra*): The seat dedicated to Bhadra, with five, seven or nine tapering quarter-circular steps erected at the south-west corner of the *kalari.*

puliangam (*puli-an-gam*): An advanced method of combating with the sword and shield, once very much a part of *kalarippayattu,* now extinct.

Rangabhyasam (*ran-gaa-bhyaa-sam*): A treatise in Malayalam on the art of warfare.

Samoothiri (*saa-moo-thi-ri*): A royal family of Calicut. Zamorin in English.

silambam (*si-lam-bam*): A Tamil word to mean the five-foot long cane or bamboo staff. Exercises done with such a staff.

Siva (*siva*): The Hindu god believed to have His abode in the highest peak of the Himalaya mountains.

swadeshi (*swa-de-shi*): Nationalist, nationalism.

swarupam (*swa-roo-pam*):The Malayalam word meaning principality.

Tacholi Othenan (*ta-cho-li, o-the-nan*): The undisputed all-time great of *kalarippayattu.* The Ballads of North Malabar are full of tales of this famous hero's deeds. After his death at an early age of thirty-two, he was deified and continues to be worshipped to this day in his birth-place called Vatakara in Malabar.

Tamil (*ta-mil*): A highly developed Dravidian language, which is now the official language of Tamil Nadu in India.

tatamura (*tha-ta-mu-ra*): A form of fighting with the sword alone, without the shield. Now extinct.

Tellicherry (*teli-che-rri*): A town in North Malabar.

thekkan pattukal (*the-kkan, paa-ttu-kal*): A collection of Ballads of Southern Kerala.

theyyam (*theyyam*): A ritualistic folk art form of Malabar where the lore and deeds of Hindu gods, warriors etc. are enacted.

thira (*thi-ra*): A ritualistic folk art form similar to *theyyam* popular in South Malabar.

thottam (*tho-ttam*): Songs sung while performing the folk-art forms of *theyyam* and *thira.*

thotukalari (*tho-tu-ka-la-ri*): A small *kalari.*

Travancore (*tra-van-cor*): The southern part of Kerala which was once ruled by the king of Trivandrum.

Tulu Nadu (*tu-lu, naa-du*): The land in Karnataka State where Tulu is spoken as a language. Tulu has no script.

Unni Archa (*unni, aar-cha*): *A* female expert in *kalarippayattu* whose deeds are part of the Ballads of North Malabar.

urumi (*uo-ru-mi*): A sword-like weapon, sharp on both edges of its flexible blade. It can be worn around one's waist as a belt.

Usanas (*uo-saa-nas*): A scholar and saint of ancient India.

vaaithaari (*vaai-thaa-ri*): Malayalam word for oral command used in *payattu* to identify each and every Phase.

val (*vaal*): Tamil and Malayalam word for sword.

Valapattanam (*vala-pa-tta-nam*): A village near Chirakkal where the Sree Bharat Kalari established in 1948 by Chirakkal T. Sreedharan Nair functions.

vallabhatta (*valla-bha-tta*): A style of *kalarippayattu.*

valppayattu (*vaal-pa-ya-ttu*): *Val* plus *payattu.* The exercises done with a sword and shield or sword alone where two atheletes wield these weapons against each other.

valvali (*vaal-va-li*): *Val* plus *Vali.* The exercises done individually where a single person wields the sword and shield aimed at imaginary opponents.

Varahamihira (*va-raa-ha-mi-hi-ra*): A scholar and saint of ancient India.

vatakkan pattukal (*va-ta-kkan, paa-ttu-kal*): A collection of Ballads of North Malabar.

vativu (*va-ti-vu*): Stance, posture.

vattenthirippu (*va-tten-thi-ri-ppu*): A style of *kalarippayattu.*

veeshal (*vee-shal*): The Malayalam word in *payattu* to mean wielding or to wield a weapon. Swinging of weapons.

velakali (*vela-ka-li*): A ritualistic martial dance popular in South Kerala, where the performers dress like traditional warriors, and wield a sword and shield simulating the movements, steps and stances employed in *kalarippayattu.*

Veluthampi Dalava (*velu-tham-pi, da-la-va*): The name of a great chief minister of Travancore (circa 1800s)

verumkai (*ve-rum-kai*): Bare hand; techniques of defending and attacking with bare hands; bare-handed.

verumkaipitutham (*ve-rum-kai-pi-tu-tham*): The last group of exercises in *kalarippayattu* where one learns bare-handed defence and attack.

vil (*vil*): Tamil and Malayalam word for bow.

Wynad (*va-ya-naad*): The hilly region of western ghats in the eastern part of Malabar.

yakshagana (*yak-sha-gaa-na*): A stylised dance-drama, similar to Kathakali, peculiar to southern region of Karnataka State.

PHASES – INDEX

(The number in brackets is that of the Phase)

PANDEERAAN VEESHAL

KETTUKARI

MUCHAN

OTTA

VALVALI

VALPPAYATTU

MARAPITICHU KUNTHA PAYATTU

VERUMKAI

(Number in brackets is that of the page.)

DODGE (Methods of Dodging)

STRIDE (Methods of Striding)

BLOCK (Methods of Blocking)

DEFENCE AND COUNTER ATTACKS

COUNTER TRICKS

THROWS, SMASH, THRUST AND BREAKS

BIBLIOGRAPHY

1. Appan Thampuran, ***Selected Esssays,*** Malayalam, 1989.

2. Balakrishnan Nair, Chirakkal T., ***Keralabhasha Ganangal - Folk Songs***, Vol. l, Malayalam, 1993.

3. Balakrishnan Nair, Chirakkal T., ***Selected Esssays***, Malayalam, 1996.

4. Gangadharan, Thikkurissi, Dr., ***Puthariyankam - A Study***, Malayalam, 1995.

5. Gautier, Francois, ***Rewriting Indian History***, English, 1996.

6. George, K.M., Dr., ***Sahithya Charithram - Prasthanangaliloote***, Malayalam, 1998.

7. Karunakaran, K.K., Dr., ***Payyannur Kolkali - An Article***, Malayalam, 1988.

8. Kurup, K.K.N., Dr., and Vijayakumar, K., ***Kalarippayat - The Martial Art of Kerala***, English, 1997.

9. Mervanji, Pervez, ***Way of the Malabar Warrior - A Movie Documentary*** on Chirakkal T.Sreedharan Nair, English, 1981.

10. Namboothiri, Vishnu, M.V., Dr., ***Poorakkali - Folklore Study***, Malayalam, 1998.

11. Namboothiri, Vishnu, M.V., Dr., ***Theyyam - A Ritual Art Form of Malabar***, Malayalam, 1998.

12. Nayar, M.K.K., ***Kathakali - Essays***, Malayalam, 1998.

13. Padmanabhan, K.K., ***Memoirs of a Disciple - An Article in the Golden Jubilee Souvenir - Sree Bharat Kalari***, Malayalam, 1999.

14. Prasad, S.R.D., ***Lectures and Papers at Seminars*** (Several), Malayalam, 1996-1999.

15. Prasad, S.R.D., ***Articles on Kalarippayattu*** (Several), Malayalam, 1994-1999.

16. Sreedhara Menon, A., ***A Survey of Kerala History***, English, 1976.

17. Sreedharan Nair, Chirakkal T., ***Articles and Radio Talks on Kalarippayattu and Allied Subjects*** (Several), Malayalam and English, 1937-1983.

18. Sreedharan Nair, Chirakkal T., ***Kalarippayattu***, Malayalam, 1963.

19. Sreedharan Nair, Chirakkal T., ***Marmadarpanam***, Malayalam, 1956.

ACKNOWLEDGEMENTS

It was while teaching *kalarippayattu* (1956/1965 at the Y.M.C.A. College of Physical Education, Madras that our father, Chirakkal T. Sreedharan Nair started working on this manual. He showed the very first handwritten manuscript to his colleague and friend, Martin H. Trieb who was the Fulbright Lecturer from America at the College. Having gone through the manuscript, Mr. Trieb thought that the book was "thorough enough to satisfy the most exacting research scholar, yet simple enough to satisfy the layman".

Back at home in retirement, the work of expanding the content was taken up in bits and pieces. Almost always at hand were Peechaali Narayanan and Vijayan, who were Father's intimate and outstanding disciples.

In 1978, Father started reworking on the final draft of this Manual. In that we collaborated with suggestions on the treatment of the subject. Many traditional Malayalam oral commands (*vaaithaaris*) were rendered in appropriate English expressions. The language of the text was edited and sometimes rewritten to make it more direct and lucid. The completed manuscript was ready.

Many years after Father's death, when we were ready to publish this Manual, we wrote a rather elaborate Introduction and got the entire set of action photographs shot.

M.A. Sadanand (Chennai), Kamala Chandrakant (Mumbai) and Vani Mantha went through the manuscript for language. Linu Kumar, Sashi Kumar, Dhanesh, Surendran, Jithesh, Ajesh and Seema (students of the Sree Bharat Kalari) posed for the photographs in this Manual. Lakshmanan, our friend and teaching colleague at the Kalari, was a constant presence during the long photo-sessions.

M. Vijayakumar, our dear friend, professional photographer and multimedia expert from Chennai, patiently shot several thousands of pictures, arranged all the final ones in sequential order in CDs and enjoyed working on this book as much as we did.

We thank everyone who helped us in making this book, *this* book.

S.R.A. DAS

S.R.D. PRASAD